GREECE

Robin Mead

GREECE

B.T. Batsford Ltd
London and Sydney

To the people of Greece

First published 1976

Made and printed in Great Britain by
Elliott Bros & Yeoman Ltd, Liverpool L24 9JL
for the publishers B.T. Batsford Ltd
4 Fitzhardinge Street, London W1H 0AH
and 23 Cross Street, Brookvale, NSW 2100, Australia

ISBN 0 7134 3080 x

Contents

GREECE
YUGOSLAVIA
ALBANIA
ITALY
MACEDONIA
Florina
Edessa
Thessalonika
Kastoria
Naoussa
Aliakmon
Mt Olympus
Thermaic Gulf
PINDUS MTS
Kalambaka
Trikala
Larisa
Pinios
THESSALY
Ioanina
Igoumenitsa
Corfu
IONIAN ISLANDS
Paxos
Preveza
Lefkas
Lamia
Thermopylea
Agrinion
Missolonghi
Nafpaktos
Delphi
Levadia
Kefalinia
Ithaca
Patras
Zakinthos
Kilini
PELOPONNESE
Corinth
Langadia
Mycenae
Epidaurus
Pyrgos
Tiryns
Nafplion
Olympia
Tripolis
ARCADIAN MTS
Proti
Kalamata
Sparta
Spetsai
Pylos
Sapientza
Schiza
Monemvasia
Cape Taineron
Kithera
MEDITERRANEAN SEA
0
50
100 miles
50
150 kms

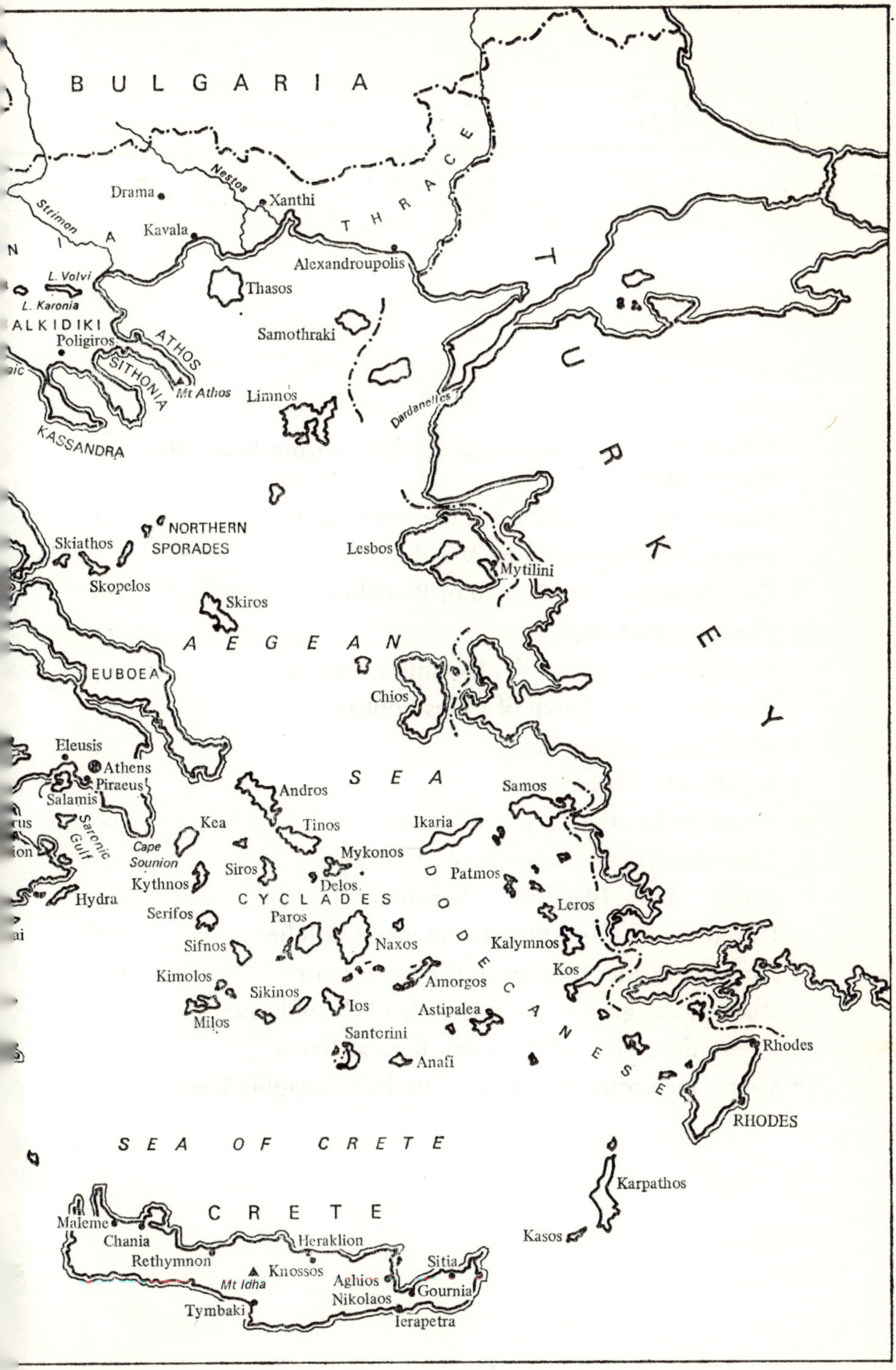
BULGARIA
THRACE
TURKEY
Nestos
Strimon
Drama
Xanthi
Kavala
Alexandroupolis
L. Volvi
L. Karonia
ALKIDIKI
Poligiros
ATHOS
SITHONIA
Mt Athos
KASSANDRA
Thasos
Samothraki
Limnos
Dardanelles
NORTHERN SPORADES
Skiathos
Skopelos
Skiros
Lesbos
Mytilini
AEGEAN SEA
EUBOEA
Chios
Eleusis
Athens
Piraeus
Salamis
Saronic Gulf
Cape Sounion
Hydra
Andros
Tinos
Kea
Kythnos
Siros
Mykonos
Delos
CYCLADES
Serifos
Sifnos
Paros
Naxos
Kimolos
Milos
Sikinos
Ios
Amorgos
Santorini
Anafi
Astipalea
Ikaria
Samos
Patmos
Leros
Kalymnos
Kos
DODECANESE
Rhodes
RHODES
SEA OF CRETE
Karpathos
Kasos
CRETE
Maleme
Chania
Rethymnon
Heraklion
Knossos
Mt Idha
Tymbaki
Aghios Nikolaos
Gournia
Sitia
Ierapetra

The Plates

1. History and Culture

THE ancient Greeks called the Mediterranean 'the road', and although the mountainous interior of the central and northern areas of the mainland is very much a part of modern Greece, just as the sprawling cities are, it is towards the hundreds of islands littered across the blue waters of the Aegean that the face of Greece is turned. This is not altogether surprising. across these waters have come both conquerors and wealth; and from these islands have come many of the most famous Greeks, from Homer down to the millionaire shipowners whose lives and loves are of such perennial interest to newspaper gossip columnists. Sooner or later almost every Greek that you meet will tell you proudly of 'my island'—the island in which his family's roots are embedded. And this, coupled with the fact that if you include Crete the Greek islands comprise one-fifth of the country's entire land area, means that the Greeks are still, in the colourless words of the textbooks, 'a maritime people'.

Greece's preoccupation with the sea is reflected not only in the country's huge merchant shipping fleet, but in the vast network of communications which links the various islands and which have ensured that, despite the geographical facts, the Greeks are not an insular people. True, the islander you meet on some remote spot in the Cyclades may never have travelled farther than the next island, or perhaps—just once—to Athens. But he, or she, will be well informed on everything from the country's contorted politics to the latest fashions in clothes and *bouzouki*-style pop music.

The visitor, still, is seen partly as a means of adding to that store of information—for Greece is only now emerging from the centuries of historical isolation and foreign domination which have encouraged people to include this essentially western nation in the boundless and mysterious world we term 'the orient'. As a result the Greeks, from the most sophisticated Athenian to the humblest worker on the land, will greet tourists with a unique mixture of friendship and curiosity. Where do you come from? What do British people think of Greece becoming a republic? Are you married? Where did you buy your jacket? How much was it? Would you like to see a photograph of my family? Do all English girls wear trousers? Do you like Greece? Those are the lines that a chance conversation with a Greek often takes—and it is often followed up with an invitation to a meal, a party, or perhaps even some local celebration such as a wedding. Greek hospitality, especially in the remoter areas, is overwhelming and embarrassing. Admire something—an ornament, a picture, or item of clothing—in a house in an island village, and you may well find the relevant item being pressed upon you as a gift. Offer to pay, and your new friendship will come to an abrupt end.

The Mediterranean is indeed 'the road' between these islands, a road as picturesque as it is rich in history. Surely one of the most beautiful sights in Europe must be the green and brown patchwork quilt of the Cyclades, set in a deep blue sea, seen from the window of an aircraft crossing from Athens to Rhodes; or a Cretan sunset turning the waters of the Gulf or Mirabello into the 'wine dark sea' that Homer described.

I have often taken my family to Greece on the Hellenic Mediterranean Lines car ferry *Egnatia*, running between Brindisi, on the heel of Italy, and the Greek port of Patras. Going east the ship crosses the Adriatic during the hours of darkness then spends the day running south past the Ionian islands, in what is as lovely a ferry trip as you will find anywhere; and my small sons have long been convinced that as the ship approaches Greece the sea turns bluer. A childish fantasy? Perhaps—but it is suggested by many experts that the waters of the Eastern Mediterranean are lacking in some of the minute plant and other life forms on which small fish feed and which give more westerly waters their greenish tinge. Whether the explanation of Greece's blue seas is scientific, or the work of one's imagination, or merely a reflection of cloudless summer skies, there is another, harsher, aspect to this optical delight: these are seas in which it is hard for the fishermen of the Aegean to make a living.

The shortages are not apparent in the coastal *tavernas*, where fish dishes feature strongly among the snacks, or *mezethes*, which Greeks take with their evening *ouzo*—the cheap, colourless local spirit which turns cloudy when water is added, tastes of aniseed, and carries an unexpected kick. Don't miss, for example, the delicious *barbounia*, or red mullet, fried and eaten whole, the *taramosalata* (fish roes), or even slices of slightly rubbery squid.

Tavernas—an individualistic mixture of restaurant, bar, and palace of varieties—are where the Greeks like to spend their evenings after a long day in the office or working in the fields. The day starts early, and is broken up by an afternoon siesta of anything up to four hours, especially in the summer when cities like Athens can become stiflingly hot. Later, if they do not go to the *taverna*, Greeks usually spend the evening with their families, for Greece is a country where family ties are still very strong. Being invited into a Greek home is a great honour—but young tourists should beware, for being asked home by a member of the opposite sex to 'meet the family' is looked upon by the older generation as notice of an impending engagement.

At weekends, or on public holidays, the gregarious city Greeks head en masse for the sea, to swim and sunbathe (one of the ways of finding a good beach near any Greek town is to follow the locals), or simply to gaze towards those distant horizons where Odysseus may have wandered and from which Greece seems to draw the very breath of life.

If Greece draws life from the sea, then our western civilisation is said to owe its origins to Greece which, despite its distinctly undemocratic postwar history, is described by historians as the birthplace of democracy. Certainly democracy, or a version of it, had a part to play in the development of the city state of Athens; but that apart, ancient Greek history is a saga of legendary deeds and wars in which fact and fiction have become inextricably intermingled. Knowledge of the flourishing and influential civilisations of Crete goes back 5,000 years to 3,000 B.C., and is now based upon solid archaeological evidence. Greek civilisation emerges about 1300 B.C., and the poems of the blind Homer, dating from the end of the eighth century or the seventh century B.C., tell of the bloodthirsty struggles between the Achaeans of Greece and the Phrygians of Troy between 1194 and 1184 B.C.—a story considered mythical until the German archaeologist Schliemann actually unearthed the foundations of Troy and Mycenae.

Just as the stories of Robin Hood have become a part of English folklore, so the old stories of the Creation, the battles between the Gods on Mount Olympus, the heroic deeds of Hercules (or, to give him his Greek name, Heracles), and the Trojan War were passed on from mouth to mouth and from generation to generation, and even partly recorded in the ancient and only recently deciphered Linear-B script. This rich store of legend was known as the 'epic cycle', and was much drawn upon by Homer as well as by later poets and dramatists. By recording these epics in composite form, Homer was unwittingly presenting historians of the future with a picture of contemporary Greek values as well as beliefs. Furthermore, he was laying the foundations of the classicism from which the writers and artists of the Renaissance—among them Botticelli, Rubens and Shakespeare—were to draw inspiration.

Greek myths and legends are a complex mixture of religious beliefs, folk tales, fables, and traditional stories which, like the tales of Troy, were based on fact. The dividing line is not always clear.

The earliest, the Olympic creation myths, bear a certain similarity to the biblical stories of the creation, with the Earth springing from an empty space known as Chaos and then giving birth to Uranus (the heavens) and Pontus (the sea). The events which followed, according to the myths, are rather less biblical. Uranus fathered (and the Earth, or Ge, mothered) such unlovable creatures as the hundred-handed giants called the Centimani, the one-eyed Cyclops, and the twelve Titans. It was not a happy family: Uranus was wounded and deposed by Cronus, the youngest of the Titans, who then married his sister Rhea but swallowed each of their children at birth in order that he should not in turn be deposed by his own son. Only Zeus, the youngest, escaped the gruesome fate because Rhea gave Cronus a stone to swallow instead and hid Zeus in the Dictaean Cave in Crete. There, according to Minoan tradition, Zeus was nursed by a goat, grew to adulthood, and was eventually able to force Cronus to disgorge his brothers and sisters. Joined by his brothers, Hades and Poseidon, Zeus then waged a ten-year war against Cronus and the other Titans, led by Atlas. Plots were followed by counter-plots, and the weapons brought into play included such fearsome innovations as Zeus's thunderbolt, but the trio eventually vanquished the Titans and sentenced Atlas to carry the sky (and not the earth, as is wrongly depicted in so many cartoons) on his shoulders as a perpetual punishment. The brothers then shared out the world, with Hades taking charge of the underworld, Poseidon taking the sea, and Zeus setting up residence in the traditional spot on the summit of Mount Olympus, in northern Greece, and ruling over the sky. On Mount Olympus, Zeus was joined by the eleven other Olympian deities: Poseidon; Hestia, goddess of the hearth fire; Demeter, goddess of agriculture; Hera, wife to Zeus; Aphrodite, the goddess of desire known to the Romans as Venus; Pallas Athene, who embodied wisdom and power; Apollo; Artemis the huntress; Hephaestus, the smith god; Ares, god of war; and Hermes. Later a newcomer, Dionysus, the wine god, was to take the place of Hestia.

The deeds of each of the Olympian deities, the story of Jason and the Argonauts, the labours of Heracles, the history of the Trojan War, the separate Cretan and Theban myths, and the wanderings of Odysseus—all are told in the ancient legends. But besides forming the basis of the people's religious beliefs and relating what was supposed to be the history of the Eastern Mediterranean world, the legends also served to explain some of the natural phenomena of the time and the area. The smoke and flame pouring from volcanic Mount Etna, in Sicily, for example was said to be due to the burial beneath the mountain of either Enceladus or Typhon, one of the enemies of Zeus.

The creation of mankind was ascribed in the legends to one of the Titans, Prometheus. Zeus, in what one may now regard as a genuine flash of divine intuition about the future misdeeds of Prometheus's creation, was sufficiently enraged to chain Prometheus to a crag in the Caucasus and instruct an eagle to tear at his liver all day long—a punishment which the unfortunate Prometheus was to endure for many years until Heracles finally shot the eagle. Soon after this point in the legends the similarity with the Old Testament stories reappears, for it was said that Zeus decided to wipe out mankind with a flood. But Prometheus's son, Deucalion, as independent and as inventive as his father, saved his family by building an ark and riding out the nine-day flood until the ark finally came to rest on Mount Parnassus. Deucalion's son, Hellen, is the mythical ancestor of all the Hellenic people.

Archaeologists give the Hellenes a rather more prosaic background. As a people they are thought to be a northern, Aryan race, equipped with horses and wheeled vehicles, who moved into Greece in the Middle Bronze Age, about 2000 B.C., and fused with the Mediterranean stock who had spread into the country a thousand years earlier and replaced the indigenous Neolithic people.

The Mediterranean peoples had long enjoyed a civilisation of their own centred upon the Cyclades islands. The Aegean is largely cut off from the rest of the Mediterranean; it is in effect an island-studded lake bounded to the north and west by the Greek mainland, to the east by Turkey, and to the south by the mountainous island of Crete. The Levantine people who had settled on Crete as early as 5000 B.C. built up in the Cyclades a peaceful trading community, for sea travel was comparatively simple and in these waters a sailor was seldom out of sight of land. Relatively prosperous, and without enemies, the Cretans built extensive and unfortified settlements at Knossos, near the present capital of the island, Heraklion, and at Phaistos in the south. In the Cyclades the islanders turned industriously to mining, and traded in copper and gems. Mariners ventured to Asia and Africa to find the tin with which copper must be combined to make bronze.

The Minoan civilisation at Knossos is named after the legendary King Minos of Crete, whose horrific bull-headed son, the Minotaur, was reputed to be kept in a labyrinth of passages through which the Athenian prince Theseus was able to find his way and kill the Minotaur only by using a reel of thread in order to be able to retrace his steps. When the archaeologist Sir Arthur Evans excavated Knossos in 1900 the ruins that he found were so extensive that he thought at first that he had discovered the legendary labyrinth, and that another of the old stories had come true. In fact, he was in the luxurious palace of Knossos, built in a style centuries ahead of its time. Light wells let in the sunshine, there were proper washing and toilet facilities, and the cellars were found to be stuffed with jars of food and wine.

These were the days of wine and roses in the Aegean. Painting, sculpture, sport—such were the pastimes of a people who had both the leisure and the wealth to indulge themselves. But nature was to intervene dramatically.

It is still not known quite what happened, or when. Perhaps this Aegean civilisation was the mysterious Atlantis, and doubtless if it had been allowed to continue the history of the entire area, and perhaps of the world, would have been very different. But, sometime between 1500 and 1300 B.C., a cataclysmic earthquake or volcanic eruption shattered the area. The clues are few and far between, but the Greek legend of Deucalion and the flood, the biblical story of the parting of the Red Sea, modern radio-carbon dating, and in the middle of the Aegean the visual evidence of the extraordinary sunken crater and still-smoking islets that make up Santorini, all point to a volcanic eruption of unimaginable proportions. Indeed, Santorini still reminds one irresistably of what it in fact is: an enormous volcanic crater peeping above the waves.

Santorini is estimated to have exploded with a force three times greater than Krakatoa, the eruption of which in 1883 killed some 36,000 people in Java and Sumatra with tidal waves, and which was heard 2,000 miles away. Santorini, then known as Thira, all but disappeared; the north coast of Crete, every Aegean island, and most ports in mainland Greece must have been devastated. Few vessels in the Mediterranean could have remained afloat, and the loss of life must have been enormous. The glorious Minoan culture, which had no enemies but nature, disappeared beneath the waves or was buried under 130 feet of volcanic ash.

The heirs to the Minoan civilisation were the warlike Mycenaeans from mainland Greece, named after their principal city, Mycenae, in the Peloponnese. Although the Mycenaeans inherited some aspects of Minoan culture, such as writing, they did not build great cities. True they built palaces, at Mycenae itself, at Tiryns, at Pylos, and on the rock of the Acropolis in Athens. But they devoted much of their time to warfare, invasion, and conquest. Syria, Cyprus, and the coastline of Asia Minor all suffered the depradations of these cruel slave-traders, and the best-known attack of all was on the city of Troy in about 1200 B.C. By this time the Greek peoples were loosely united under Mycenaean rule, and their king, Agamemnon, led the expedition against Troy from which grew one of the last, and perhaps the greatest,

1 Athens: looking towards the Parthenon from beside the Erechtheum

of the Greek legends. Twelve hundred ships are said to have taken part in the siege of Troy, and the eventual capture of the city by means of a ruse—hiding Greek soldiers in a wooden horse presented to the Trojans—is a story which we still learn as children. It is also the incident which gave rise to the popular expression which, even today, Hellenic people regard as an insult: 'Beware of Greeks bearing gifts.'

But the Trojan War, coupled with internal strife, undermined the strength of the Mycenaeans and brought their civilisation to almost as abrupt an end as its predecessor. Towards the end of the twelfth century B.C. new invaders, the Dorians, a semi-barbarous people armed with iron swords, swept down from what are now Bulgaria and Yugoslavia, sacking Pilos and Tiryns, and burning Mycenae. Only the Acropolis in Athens escaped the destruction. The Dorians were not interested in art, writing, architecture, or even trade; they lived by conquest and destruction.

Eventually, however, invaders and invaded were to mingle and merge. The Dorians' iron tools revolutionised farming, and in places like Sparta and Corinth there were established self-supporting independent city states governed by the men who had the wealth or the strength to subdue and hold the surrounding area. From these city-states, adventurers once again set sail to explore and colonise the Aegean world and beyond. Settlements grew up on parts of the Black Sea coastline, in Libya, Sicily, southern Italy, and even as far afield as the coasts of France and Spain. The Italians invented a word for these settlers from the east: Greeks.

At home, things were changing fast and new ideas were developing. Religion, based upon the worship of the gods on Mount Olympus, was widespread, and the religious centres at Olympia, Delphi, and Eleusis attracted a considerable following. Writing returned to the country, although the new Greek

2 *Athens: the Acropolis from the south-west*

alphabet was Phoenician, and philosophy, poetry and science all reappeared.

Athens, which was well placed geographically and was surrounded by fertile land, grew and prospered. On top of the rock of the Acropolis the Athenians had built a magnificent temple to the goddess Athene, after whom the city was named. But the grandeur of this magnificent structure disguised a simmering discontent over the gulf which had arisen between the rich farm owners and the peasants. The only law was the one decreed by the aristocrats, and it fell to one of these aristocrats, Solon, to introduce a radical programme of reform in about 590 B.C. Solon's innovations included a 400-member governing council for the city drawn from all classes, and the establishment of courts and the jury system. Democracy had been born.

It was a short-lived reform. When Solon retired, the new schemes were quickly dropped by the aristocracy, who again seized power. But the poorer classes, having had a taste of freedom, rebelled and elected their own leader, Peisistratus, in about 560 B.C. giving him the powers of *tyrant*, a Greek work meaning king in all but name. Peisistratus governed Athens well for 20 years; under his guidance the city prospered as a commercial and financial centre, money having been introduced into Greece from Asia Minor. Gold and silver were mined in Greece under Athenian guidance, and the city became the leader of the Greek city states. Its only rival was Sparta, in the Peloponnese, where the mainly Dorian people were still poor but had all the pride and toughness of their ancestors. Sparta was the only part of Greece to create and maintain a standing army, training boys and young men to a harsh, military way of life which was truly 'Spartan'.

After the death of Peisistratus there was a brief period of turmoil in Athens before the people elected a new leader, Cleisthenes, a political reformer who attempted to expand upon the democratic innovations of Solon and who is today credited with being the first leader to introduce democratic government. Cleisthenes introduced the principles by which every free Greek citizen could attend an assembly of the people and discuss city affairs, and a new 500-member ruling council was set up, its members being elected by the people.

Meanwhile, in the Middle East, a new power had arisen: Persia. Under the wise leadership of King Cyrus the Great, Persia had established a sphere of influence which stretched from India to Asia Minor, and the Persian policy was that these places should be granted a large measure of self-government. One of Cyrus's successors, Darius, had added to the Persian empire by conquering large areas of south-eastern Europe, including Macedonia. But at the beginning of the fifth century B.C. some Ionian cities revolted against Persian overlordship and asked Athens and the city of Eretria, on the island of Euboea, north-east of Athens, for help. Athens and Eretria sent an expeditionary force to help the rebels, and this force attacked and razed the Persian provincial capital of Sardis. It was a lone success, for the revolt was crushed and Persian anger was directed against Greece. Envoys sent to Athens and Sparta were executed and Darius, who made a servant repeat to him every night the words: 'Remember the Athenians', began to prepare an army of revenge to lay siege to Athens. The anxious Athenians asked Sparta and the other city-states for help, but they all declined. The one exception was little Plataea, which offered 1,000 men.

Darius did not go in for any half measures. His army of 40,000 men in 600 vessels sacked Eretria, burned its temples, and carried off the entire population as prisoners, as retribution for the burning of Sardis. Darius planned to punish Athens in the same way. Only 10,000 Athenian citizen-soldiers, plus the contingent from Plataea, stood between the city and the formidable Persian force.

The Persians cannot have expected the tiny Greek army to attack, expecially as they had no bowmen and were armed principally with spears. But attack they did, and thanks to their enthusiasm for athletics the Greeks were very fit. What is more they were desperate, and desperate men can work wonders. Unable to manoeuvre the Persians gave ground, and a final attack by two Greek squadrons of cavalry threw the invaders into confusion. Before evening they were retreating towards their ships and the following Greeks captured seven vessels. It proved to be a memorable victory, for the Greeks lost 192 dead, against Persian losses of no less than 6,400 men. A Greek athlete, Pheidippides, was despatched to Athens, 26 miles away to announce the victory. He ran all the way, gasped out his message, then collapsed and died—an incident still commemorated in the Marathon race at today's Olympic Games.

Persia had been defeated, but a long-standing enmity had begun. Even Sparta, which regretted its part in killing one of Darius' messengers and sent two volunteers to his court to apologise and offer their lives in retribution, could not heal the breach. When they arrived Darius was dead, but his son, Xerxes, sent them home with the warning that Sparta could not escape the burden of its guilt by offering Persia the chance of reprisals.

In 481 B.C., Xerxes was ready. A huge army said to number five million men, although historians are divided on this point, was marshalled at the Hellespont, the modern-day Dardanelles. When this army crossed the straits and began its march along the coastline of northern Greece, the Persian navy supported it with supplies. The Greeks, despite having had ample warning of the invasion, were unprepared because of disagreements between the city-states, but they had built a fleet of about 200 ships which assembled in Piraeus, the harbour of Athens. They also had another strong card in their hands, for this time the Spartans were on their side. Leonidas, the King of Sparta, took personal command of the Spartan troops and of the 20,000-strong Greek army. But, despite the threat of attack, it was the season for the Olympic Games in Greece, the regular sporting event during which war and fighting were considered improper. As the Persians reached Thermopylae Sparta sent just 300 middle-aged men, under Leonidas, to defend the vital pass, promising that the rest would join them after the games were over. Leonidas bravely tackled the Persian army on the vital road leading to Southern Greece.

In the epic two-day battle the slaughter was terrible. The Persians, hampered by their great numbers, trampled each other in their efforts to get at the 300 enemy. The Spartans fought with spears, swords, then with their fists and teeth. But the battle could only end one way, and the Spartans perished.

The battle was, of course, no more than an irritant to the invading Persians, who swept on. But the Spartans' heroism inspired the Greeks. Their navy engaged the Persian fleet, and inflicted considerable losses. But Athens had to be evacuated as the Persians advanced, and the invaders set fire to the buildings on the Acropolis. The Greeks retreated to the Isthmus of Corinth, where their fleet was able to attack and destroy the Persian fleet. Unable to obtain supplies, Xerxes was forced to retreat into Thessaly, and thus gave the Greeks a valuable breathing space. The next year the Persians again attacked Plataea, but found the Greeks prepared and suffered a severe defeat. This land victory was followed by a naval battle near Samos, which the Greeks also won. The Persians retreated, and for the next 30 years the warfare between the two countries became intermittent and of a guerrilla nature. It was not until 450 B.C. that both sides agreed not to attack one another.

Although Persian power had been broken, Athens had not benefited from the war morally. Instead of championing Greek freedom Athens, with its powerful fleet, became the overlord of a country which once more centred itself on the Aegean. There was still a lack of unity between Athens and Sparta, the greatest land force. Power in Athens had passed to a warrior named Cimon, but his attempts to unite the city-states of Greece into a loose military union called the Delian League proved unpopular and he was accused of being pro-Spartan.

Cimon was succeeded by one of the greatest Athenian leaders, Pericles, who was very popular with the people and became virtual head of the Athenian state. His leadership brought to Athens a period of calm which enabled the city to rebuild its strength. He insisted that Athens should be the leader of the

Delian League, and indeed the city's wealth and naval power was such that the city-states gradually became absorbed into the Athenian empire. At the same time democracy within the city was improved, with greater public participation, Sculpture and architecture flourished, and the Elgin marbles—which decorated the Parthenon and are now in the British Museum—were executed during this period. The drama of Sophocles and Euripides became popular, and schools of thinkers also developed, with Socrates being one of the best known philosophers of the time. Socrates' most famous pupil was Plato; Plato in turn was to teach Aristotle; and Aristotle was to become tutor to a young Macedonian prince called Alexander who was to make his own dramatic mark on the world.

This magnificent era ended with the death of Pericles and the second Peloponnesian War between Athens and Sparta—a prolonged and intermittent struggle which did not end until the eventual defeat of the Athenians by Sparta in 405 B.C. Sparta, now the dominant state, ruled its new empire with a harsh hand, but during all this renewed inter-state rivalry the kingdom of Macedonia, in northern Greece, was watching and waiting its chance to exploit the situation.

In 338 B.C., King Philip of Macedonia attacked southern Greece and took control of the entire country. He attempted to restore peace and culture to the country, but in vain. He also turned his military attentions towards the old enemy, Persia, but before he could launch the attack he planned he was assasinated, and his 20-year-old son, Alexander, ascended the throne.

There was a rapid series of revolts against what Athenians were calling 'merely a crazy boy', but the rebels of Thebes and the north were quickly crushed and then, with a powerful army of 35,000 men, the man who was to be called Alexander the Great crossed the Hellespont, freed Troy, and met the Persian army at Granicus. Alexander's troops scattered the Persians, although Alexander himself narrowly escaped death. Alexander then resolved to break Persian sea power by marching round to

Egypt and capturing every enemy port on the way. En route he stopped at the Temple of Gordium, where a complicated knot was reputed to hold the key to a continent. Whoever could untie the knot would rule Asia, it was said. Alexander sliced the knot in half with one stroke of his sword.

An attempt by the Persian king, Darius III, to stop Alexander's advance was broken at Issus, and Darius wrote to Alexander offering him one third of his empire. Alexander spurned the offer, replying: 'You must address me as Supreme Lord of all Asia. If you claim your kingdom, stand and fight for it.'

Tyre, Gaza, and the Egyptian capital of Memphis all fell to Alexander. And on the Nile delta Alexander founded his own port, Alexandria. The 25-year-old monarch marched on to Libya, then turned back into Mesopotamia to meet a new challenge from Darius who now had a heavily-equipped army including 200 chariots and some war elephants from India. Brilliant leadership enabled Alexander to break this Persian force at Gaugamela. Victorious, Alexander marched on unopposed to Babylon, at that time the greatest city in the world, and then to the rich and legendary Persian capitals of Susa, Persepolis, and Ecbatana. The gold which Alexander captured he ordered to be turned into coins, which he and his men quickly spent.

There seemed to be no end to Alexander's wanderings. Although he now had the throne of Persia in his grasp, he marched on to western India, and might well have continued to the borders of China if disturbances in Persia had not compelled him to return to Babylon. There Greece, Macedonia and Persia were formally united when Alexander married a Persian princess, Roxana. But, while at Babylon, Alexander became ill—probably with marlaria—and he died in 323 B.C.

Had he lived, Alexander could have brought peace to the Middle East. In fact his only natural heir, the child Roxana was carrying, was to be assassinated very quickly, and Alexander's own deathbed wish was that his kingdom should go 'to the strongest'. As a result his empire was divided between three Macedonian generals. Ptolemy took Egypt, and at once declared his independence from the rest; Seleucus took the Asian territories apart from the lands on the Indian border where there had already been a revolt; and Kassandros became King of Greece and its European colonies. The divisions, rivalries and conquests which followed were to last until Greece became part of the Roman Empire.

Ptolemy proved to be the strongest of Alexander's successors, and the centre of Hellenic culture moved to Alexandria. Ptolemy's empire grew to include Libya, Palestine, and Cyprus, and the magnificent lighthouse which he had built at the entrance to Alexandria harbour became one of the ancient wonders of the world.

In 280 B.C., the divided Greek mainland was once again threatened by the barbaric hordes to the north. Gauls from the Danube region swept into Macedonia, and Alexander the Great's homeland crumpled under their attack. The city-states of central Greece banded together to meet the aggressors, and once again decided to make a stand at the vital pass of Thermopylae. But the Gallic King, Brennus, rounded the pass and plunged on towards the religious centre of Delphi. In previous times of national crisis the mysterious Delphic oracle had not always proved accurate, or perhaps it was just that the oracle's enigmatic prophecies were misunderstood. This time, the oracle seemed as vague as ever. 'Let the Barbarians come' commanded the voice which was said to speak for Apollo. 'The care for these things falls on me, and the white maidens'.

The Gauls came on, although their numbers became fewer as contingents broke off to raid villages and towns along the way. Only a few thousand Greeks were available to meet the apparently unstoppable horde as they fell upon Delphi. After a day-long battle, Brennus and his army decided to spend the night in the deep gorge below the shrine. And then, in one of the most dramatic moments in the drama-filled history of Greece, the 'white maidens' arrived—a thickening storm of snowflakes which strong winds swept into heavy drifts. The Gauls awoke to a blizzard, and as they slipped and slithered their way back up towards the shrine the Greeks fell upon them. The Gauls were scattered and destroyed, and only one-third of the original attacking force got out of the country alive.

Meanwhile, Pyrrhus, a Greek general who was a cousin of Alexander the Great, was in southern Italy, attempting to defend the Greek enclaves there against the power of an emergent Rome. He found to his surprise that he was up against a huge force of well-drilled and heavily-armoured men, and although he scored some early successes against the Romans, Pyrrhus found that the cost was too great—they were Pyrrhic victories. He returned to Greece where Sparta, which shared many of the Roman ideals, had already forged a link with Rome.

Fascinated by Greek culture, appalled by the country's internal decay, and feeling itself threatened by the halfhearted Greek attempts to play at power politics in the Mediterranean vacuum, Rome finally decided to protect the Greeks both from outside aggressors and from themselves. A powerful army under Flamininus won two victories over the Greeks, and in 196 B.C. Flamininus officially announced that Rome was now 'the protector of Greece. When there was a revolt against Roman rule 50 years later, Corinth was levelled by Roman troops as an example to the rest of the country. The Greeks were forced to accept the ineveitable as the Roman Emperor, Augustus, imposed the 'Peace of Rome' all the way from Britain to Babylon.

It was at this moment in time that Christ was born in Bethlehem, and it is worth recalling that as Greek was the common language of the eastern Mediterranean at this time, Jesus must have known and used Greek. But, despite the faith which the Apostle Paul, a Hellenised Jew, was to bring to Asia Minor, Thessaly, Athens, and finally Corinth (where he formed a Christian community), it took 300 years for Christianity to take firm root in the Eastern Mediterranean. While Christians were still being martyred in Rome, Roman emperors like Hadrian were worshipping the pagan Greek gods. Hadrian, a Grecophile, built in Athens both a library and a clocktower called the Tower of the Winds which still stands in the centre of the city.

The religious breakthrough came when the Emperor Constantine was converted to Christianity, and granted Christians religious freedom. To this day Constantine, who died in 337, is known to Greeks as the founding father of the Orthodox Greek world. Fittingly the city which Constantine had built seven years before his death on the site of old Byzantium, on the western shore of the Bosphorus dividing Europe and Asia, was to become a place to which Greeks would always look both with love and pride. He called it Constantinople.

Constantinople, founded by a Roman but essentially an eastern city, flourished throughout the dark ages of Europe, an oasis of culture. Missionaries and teachers ventured into the Balkans and Russia, taking with them both a new alphabet and a new religion. The Byzantines—as the people under Constantinople's sway were called—made mosaic pictures with bits of glass embedded in wet plaster, a classic art form of which good examples can still be found in Constantinople (now called Istanbul), Ravenna in Italy, and at Daphni near Athens. Byzantine artists also practised fresco painting, the art form which was to spark the Italian Renaissance. Religious feelings were also expressed in small painted wooden panels called *icons*, the Greek word for 'images', which can still be found in the Eastern Mediterranean.

Although it was a peaceful city, interested mainly in literature, the arts, learning, architecture and religion, Constantinople could be aroused to anger. When the Persians and the wild tribes of Eurasia captured Jerusalem and carried off the Christians' holiest relic, the True Cross, the Emperor Heraclius quickly gathered an army and set out to recover it. In a campaign similar to that of Alexander the Great he stormed into Persia and recaptured the Cross in 628.

With the collapse of the Roman Empire, Byzantium had become a largely Greek-speaking entity centred on Greece and the Eastern Mediterranean. The region in general, and Constantinople in particular, were the scene of a series of power struggles and intrigues, and by the year 1000 Byzantium was surrounded by enemies, with the Bulgars to the north, the emergent Saracens to the east and south, and its trading rival Venice in the west. The Emperor Basil broke Bulgar power in a savage battle, and a successor, Alexius I, beat off another attack, this time by Norman invaders from the west.

Alexius welcomed the First Crusade against the Turks, but rather than being its saviour, the Crusades were to be the death of Byzantium. In the year 1204 the Venetians diverted the Fourth Crusade, orignally aimed at the Holy Land, and hurled it against Constantinople. The city's gigantic and supposedly impregnable walls were breached, and the city was sacked. During three days of pillaging and looting, the work of 800 years was undone.

Broken, Byzantium was divided into feudal states which did not last. Amazingly, there was a resurgence of Byzantine power when Michael Palaeologus recaptured Constantinople in 1261, and Byzantine culture was briefly reborn. But the revived empire was already doomed, because the trade routes which had been the city's arteries were now blocked, or dominated by other states. In 1453 the Ottoman Turk Mohammed II lay siege to Constantinople, and aroused hardly a murmur of protest from the rest of the world. Although foreign ships and their crews volunteered to help defend the city, Sultan Mohammed's troops were armed with cannons which breached the city walls. Mohammed took the city, and marched on to capture Athens in 1456.

Although they were not cruel masters, the Turks did treat the Greeks as second-class citizens. Under Turkish rule large Christian families had to give one son to the Turks to be brought up as a janissary—a group which formed an élite corps of Turkish troops. But the prophet Mohammed had ordered that his followers should allow religious freedom to Jews and Christians, so the Greek religion did not die.

Greek culture was also kept alive, and fittingly enough Venice, which had played a major part in the downfall of Byzantium, helped by giving asylum to many Greek intellectuals and classicists who fled. Only when the Ottoman Turks overreached themselves did things begin to change on mainland Greece, however. In 1664 the Austrians beat the Turks decisively in a battle at St Gotthard. Venice saw its chance and overran the Peloponnese and Attica, and it was during this campaign that the Parthenon in Athens was partially destroyed–a Venetian shell falling into the temple which the Turks were using as a gunpowder magazine.

In the Greek heartland, where the population had been declining steadily for centuries, Greek Christian brigands hiding out in the mountains were beginning to make their presence felt. The Turks were forced to stop recruiting Greek children for the janissary corps, and as the Turkish military position declined so the Greeks took greater control of the commercial and political life of their country. Although the Turks now treated their Greek subjects as near equals, however, they were not going to give up their empire without a fight. In the eighteenth century Turkish troops recaptured the Peloponnese, and even Russian intervention on behalf of the people with whom they had Orthodox religious ties was to no avail.

But the social order was changing; the French Revolution stirred the hearts of the oppressed Greek people, and although at the Congress of Vienna the leaders of the great European powers agreed to shore up the crumbling Ottoman empire, Greek independence was becoming inevitable. On the 25 March 1821, Archbishop Germanos of Patras officially proclaimed Greek independence, and the date is still celebrated as Greece's National Day.

There was immediate communal bloodshed, the echoes of which reverberate around the Eastern Mediterranean to this day. With the Peloponnese and many of the islands in Greek hands, there was fighting between the Turks and Greek and Albanian 'rebels' in the mountains of north western Greece. The western powers once more looked on with indifference as bitter guerrilla warfare was waged in the wilder parts of Greece, and on the waters of the Adriatic and Aegean where superior Greek seamanship played havoc with Turkish communications. This was the time when men like Goethe, Schiller, and Victor Hugo spoke out boldly for the Greek cause, and when Lord Byron dreamed aloud 'that Greece might still be free'. But Greece needed the support of arms not words, and Turkish patience was exhausted. An Egyptian mercenary, Mehemet Ali Pasha, was despatched with powerful sea and land forces to settle the issue. He seized Crete, then landed an army of 10,000 men on the Peloponnese. Greek resistance was crushed, and only the west coast port of Missolonghi–now a quiet fishing village–held out. Among the defence forces was the volunteer Byron, who died there of a fever. When the Turks finally broke through Missolonghi's defences, the townspeople blew themselves up rather than surrennder, and at last–too late–Great Britain, France, and Russia were moved to act. In 1827 a combined fleet sailed into Greek waters with the intention of forcing Mehemet's son, Ibrahim, to withdraw and to aid the creation of a Greek state. Ibrahim chose to fight at a place called Navarino Bay, but this time he had met his match. The allied fleet went into action on 27 October, sank 60 of Ibrahim's ships without loss to themselves, and the Greek Revolution was over.

International power politics led to a certain amount of argument over precisely what the new Greek state should comprise. The country's first leader, John Capodistrias, a former Russian Foreign Minister born on Corfu, settled the issue with some smart internal land grabbing which eventually led to the international recognition of a Greece made up of the Peloponnese, central Greece, and the Cyclades islands. Thessaly and Crete remained under Turkish rule, and Corfu was a British Protectorate. Even then, the rebirth of Greece was a painful affair. Many peasants, heavily over-taxed, paid the new Greek government the ultimate insult of emigrating to Turkish lands; and Capodistrias was to die the victim of an assassin's bullet.

The European powers then chose a seventeen-year-old Bavarian

Prince, Otho, to rule Greece, and he arrived in the country in 1833 with his own 'police force' of 3,500 Bavarian troops. At least this force was able to crush the armed bands which had been roaming the country and imposing their own 'rule', and they also managed to evict the remnants of the Turkish forces from Athens and make it the Greek capital once again. Constitutional monarchy was established in 1843, but there was a brief hiatus when Greece followed its age-old habit of embarking upon some dangerous international power politics, which turned the British against Otho. Otho abdicated, and in 1863 a Danish prince, George, was crowned George I, King of the Hellenes—a title which firmly established the Greek claim to Greek-speaking lands beyond their borders.

To mark the accession of George, and their approval, the British ceded Corfu and the other Ionian islands to Greece. George forced upon the country a more democratic constitution, introduced full male suffrage and the secret ballot, and broke up the great estates. But the country remained poverty-stricken, and Greeks continued to emigrate. What is more, the Great Powers were still worried about the direction in which Greece would lean. When Crete at last threw out the Turks the island was refused permission to unite with Greece, and feelings ran so high that there was almost a civil war. It fell to the politician Eleutherios Venizelos to dabble in the murky waters of international diplomacy in search of a solution. Through a succession of Balkan alliances, he was able to persuade the Great Powers to recognise both Crete and the island of Samos as Greek territory.

In 1913, the long reign of King George ended in another assassination, and Crown Prince Constantine, former Commander in Chief of the Greek army, came to the throne. But Constantine was married to a sister of the German Kaiser, Wilhelm, and also had a great professional respect for Germany's military power. As the First World War loomed, Constantine decided to play safe and side with Germany; Venizelos, who disagreed, was dismissed.

The country was split. Venizelos set up a rival government in Thessalonika, and with Allied help strong pressure was put on King Constantine. He retreated to Switzerland, and Venizelos quickly threw Greece into the war on the side of the Allies. At the Versailles Peace Conference, Venizelos earned his reward: a Greek enclave at Smyrna, on Turkey's Aegean coast, which Venizelos hoped would be a refuge for Greeks in that area. The idea was to prove disastrous. As a result of a national plebiscite King Constantine returned to Greece, and decided to make up for past failures by launching a full-scale attack upon Turkey from the base at Smyrna. The Greek army suffered a shattering defeat and lost 50,000 men, whilst the enraged Turks turned upon the Greeks living in Anatolia and slaughtered them. Smyrna was captured, sacked and burned. King Constantine abdicated, an army junta seized power in Athens, then Venizelos was asked to pick up the pieces.

Once again Venizelos showed his mastery of the art of diplomacy. At a remarkable meeting in Switzerland, Greeks and Turks agreed to settle their differences by an exchange of population. About 1,250,000 Greeks in Anatolia were to return to Greece; 400,000 Turks were to leave Greek territory for Turkey. Despite the human problems which this involved, the exchange worked well, and Venizelos returned triumphantly to the office to Prime Minister. Only another army coup was to displace him, and he died in exile in 1936.

The new leader of Greece was an army general called Ioannis Metaxas, a dictator who modelled himself on Mussolini. But he was a man of far greater mettle than the Italian fascist leader, and he carefully avoided aligning Greece with the other fascist powers. After the Italian seizure of Albania in 1940 he seemed unmoved, and even attended a party at the Italian legation in Athens. Early next day, 28 October, the Italian Ambassador called unexpectedly at his home and Metaxas, wearing only a bathrobe, opened the door himself. The Ambassador asked for formal permission for Italian troops to cross into Greece, a move which would have linked Greece inextricably with Germany and Italy. Gently, General Metaxas shook his head. '*Ochi*' ('No'), he said, then shut the door in the Ambassador's face. It was a moment which Greeks still love to recall, and 28 October is now a national festival known as 'Ochi day',

When the inevitable fighting began, the highly-regarded Italian army proved no match for the Greek forces and was forced back into the Albanian mountains. Only the intervention of powerful German forces saved the Italians from a humiliating defeat, and in the spring of 1941 the Germans completed their occupation of Greece. The Greeks responded with savage guerrilla warfare, in which they had had long practice. The Germans in turn ordered the mass execution of civilian hostages. Fighting was particularly severe in remote spots like the mountains of Crete, where even to this day German tourists receive a cool welcome in many villages.

But, as German power waned and defeat grew nearer, the Greek resistance fighters turned against each other. Half of them remained loyal to the Crown, but a strong Communist faction gained the upper hand and for a time at the end of the Second World War it looked as though Greece might be among the countries which were to disappear behind the Iron Curtain. British troops were forced to intervene to prevent the fall of Athens, and there was a massive influx of American arms and money. The Communist powers finally decided to abide by the Yalta Agreement, which placed Greece and Turkey firmly in the western sphere of influence, and Yugoslavia acted decisively by closing its border to the rebels. In 1949 the Civil War finally ended—but in terms of lives it had been more costly to Greece than the whole of the Second World War.

Today, Greek rivalries live on—partly as a result of recent history, but partly, no doubt, because of long memories and

3 Athens: the Tower of the Winds

the fiery Greek temperament. In the north, and in big cities like Thessalonika, the left is still vociferous. In Athens, the villages of the Peloponnese, and in the islands the people are more interested in the virtues of peace and prosperity than in politics. In five thousand years, this part of the world has seen too much strife.

History has left it's mark. A Greek will quickly offer you his friendship, but it will be many years before he offers you his heart. Apparently logical and philosophical, the people still put pride before reason; passions run high, and anger is not far below the surface if a Greek feels that he, or his country, is being insulted.

True anger, however, bears no relation to the daily slanging matches which the visitor will see between drivers, or between waiters and their customers. It often seems impossible to ask for directions, or even ask the time, in Greece without attracting a crowd who will offer conflicting advice, shout, and wave their arms about. Few Greeks will admit that they do not know the answer to a question, which may account for the conflicting advice.

However friendly they may appear to western visitors, the Greeks feel, with some justification, that history has misused them, and that when they try to justify their claim to the Hellenic world—which, of course includes both the island of Cyprus and large chunks of Turkey—nobody understands them. Hellenism is an emotive subject to Greeks everywhere.

And yet, despite apparently expansionist intentions, Greece is, essentially, a country of peace—a peace which today can be found in the vastness of its mountains, or on the islands scattered over the glittering seas. Its people will not expect you to know their history or to understand their problems, any more than they will expect you to know their language—although they will be delighted if you try. Their civilisation is not our civilisation, and

4 *Cape Sounion: the Temple of Poseidon*

they put different values on different things. Not least of these is that mysterious Greek entity known as 'business'—something for which the Greeks have shown a remarkable capacity during the last hundred years. But what exactly is the 'business' which apparently involves so many hours of earnest discussion over the coffee cups? Trying to find the answer to that may demonstrate just how hard it is to get to know the Greeks.

Recently, a British girl who has a Greek boyfriend was staying with him on an island off the coast of Attica when he announced that he would have to go to Athens next day on business. 'Oh good,' said the girl, 'I would like to go back to Athens to do some shopping. I will come with you.' 'You can't do that', said her Greek boyfriend. 'I'm going on business.' 'What business?' asked the girl. 'Just business' came the reply. 'But *what* business?' persisted the girl. And, in exasperation, the Greek finally turned upon her and gave what he obviously considered to be a complete explanation. 'In Greece', he said sternly 'business is *business*'.

2. Athens

THE road from Eleusis to Athens, the ancient sacred way, and every step is illustrated by ancient history . . . you may conceive our emotions as we rode along the sacred way; the monastery of Daphni appearing in view, while we knew well that, a little beyond on a rising hill, we should see the object of the greatest attraction to us in Greece, for which we had defied so many inconveniences and dangers. We knew not whether to go fast or slow. The guide determined. Suddenly he rode extremely quick—and we were obliged to follow. Athens appeared.

So wrote H. W. Williams in *Travels in Italy, Greece, and the Ionian Islands*, published in Edinburgh in 1820 and arguably the best travel book about Greece ever written. Quite by accident, I happened to approach Athens for the first time by road along the same route—the old, classic route from the west that is now a modern motorway. All the way from Corinth, where the famous canal gashes through the rock, travellers have the sea on their right, and as you look at the dazzling mixture of colours—blue sea, reddish brown rocks, and sand that is almost white—you realise that it is true, the light *is* different in Greece. It becomes as a shock when this beautiful landscape along the Gulf of Eleusis, and the clarity of the atmosphere, are both broken by the smoking chimneys of the once historic, and now predominantly industrial, town of Eleusis.

Then the road turns inland, climbs the gentle slope of Mount

Aigaleos, and passes the fortified monastery of Daphni with its rich Byzantine treasures. The traffic thickens, and below you—to echo the laconic words of H. W. Williams—Athens appears.

It is at this moment that one's heart almost misses a beat, for this first view of Athens has no equal in Europe. Rising above the rooftops, dominating the skyline, is the rock of the Acropolis. And this in turn is crowned by the white, sunlit columns of the Parthenon, easily distinguishable from many miles away.

Modern methods of transport have not cheated visitors of this first breathtaking view of Athens, unless perhaps they arrive by coach or car on the road from the north. Aircraft dipping below the hills which cluster round the city usually offer their passengers a glorious panorama of Athens and its suburbs; while as their ship ties up in the Piraeus, port of Athens, seaborne travellers can also see the Acropolis in the distance as well as the neighbouring Mount Lycabettus, another hill in the heart of the city but this time conical in shape and topped by a tiny chapel.

Sights (or one could just as correctly say sites) such as these abound in Athens, and classical ruins are ten a penny. So much so, in fact, that it is often the more modern attractions which visitors want to see first. Shopping is excellent, and the pavement restaurants a constant novelty and delight. The monarchy has gone, but the white-skirted royal guards—the Evzones—still stamp their pompom-tipped boots in unison outside the palace to the accompanying clicks of countless camera shutters.

Within the boundaries roughly imposed by the Acropolis and Mount Lycabettus, Athens seems to have crammed both past and present. The traffic sweeps past the toppled columns of the classic age and into Syntagma—or Constitution Square—which with the Parliament building on one side and ringed by most of the important airline offices and two of the eight 'Luxury' grade hotels in Athens is both a tourist and a political centre. In the square itself, the local *cafenions* which play such an important part in the capital's social life have set up tables and chairs and, when the weather demands it, shelter from the sun or from less friendly elements, and Greeks and tourists alike gather there at all hours of the day and night to talk over cool drinks, sweet Turkish-style coffee, or other refreshments. Despite the setting, the *cafenions* are not expensive.

Even cheaper are the roadside kiosks which, magically, seem to stock almost everything that a passer-by might need—from newspapers and magazines to belts and shoelaces, from sweets and tobacco to strings of 'worry beads', and from salty-tasting pistacchio nuts to postage stamps or souvenirs of the city. Like the *cafenions*, the kiosks stay open until all hours, and they perform a double role in that local telephone calls can be made from them. The ubiquitous kiosks are as much a part of Athens—or, indeed, of any major Greek city—as the roast chestnut vendors on every street corner, or the lottery ticket salesmen, carrying sticks festooned with tickets like the flags of a ship dressed overall, who appear wherever there is a crowd.

And everywhere, of course, there are the Greeks themselves—arguing, gesticulating, smiling. Greeks love life in all its aspects. They work hard and they play hard. The claim by the Greek Tourist Office that 'one hardly ever comes across a bored or surly Greek' is a truism, for despite the somnolent image which they are sometimes given overseas, they are an animated people who somehow manage to convey the impression that they are doing everything for the first time—and doing it enthusiastically.

Although the newer parts of the city are laid out in grid fashion, and there is no shortage of landmarks, Athens is surprisingly difficult to find one's way about in at first. This is partly because of the size of the city, partly because of the very un-grid-like layout of the maze of old streets around the Acropolis, and partly because the name of a street as its appears on a map, or even on the street signs, and the name by which it is known to the Athenians can be two very different things. Just when you think that you have got your bearings, you discover that you are lost—and some maps of Athens do not help matters by printing east at the top.

Apart from Constitution Square, the other main hub of Athens is Omonia, a rather less dignified square at the bottom of Venizelou Street which links the two and which contains the grand trio of buildings which house the National Library, Athens University, and the Athens Academy. A number of bed-and-breakfast style hotels, much used by inclusive tour operators, cluster around Omonia and its fountains, and the square is also the terminus of the underground railway which links Athens to Piraeus and which is by far the cheapest means of transport to and from the port area. In the streets around Omonia, crammed with traffic and a nightmare to drive in, there is a typical cross-section of the rather cheaper shops, interspersed with bars, shoe shine stalls, and stands selling *souvlaki* (grilled meat on a skewer). The charcoal-grilled *souvlaki* is always safe to eat and quite delicious. Incidentally, the water in Athens is quite safe too—in fact it is one of the purest supplies of any European city.

In the evening especially, wandering through the streets is one of the pleasures of Athens—and the shops are tempting at any time of the day. But eventually one is inevitably drawn to the Acropolis, its stones worn smooth by countless visitors.

The four remaining buildings on top of the Acropolis all date from the period between 448 and 400 B.C., and the most famous of them is the Parthenon, a temple dedicated to the goddess Athena, whose white marble columns still dominate the Greek capital as well as adorning a myriad of picture postcards. It was partially destroyed by an explosion, the details of which were given in the last chapter, and much of the sculptural decoration—executed under Phidias—was rescued from further destruction by Lord Elgin in the nineteenth century and moved to the British Museum where the 'Elgin Marbles' are now one of the prime attractions.

Architecturally the temple is interesting because, despite appearances, it does not contain any straight lines. The towering fluted Doric columns, seventeen on either side and eight at each end, in fact lean slightly inwards (an effect which can be seen from either end of the two great colonnades), and the entablature is three inches higher in the middle than at its ends. These 'deliberate mistakes' by the designer, Ictinus, in fact give the building a rare visual symmetry, and in the days when the exterior sculptural decorations were complete, and the temple itself was filled with the priceless spoils of Athenian victories in war, the Parthenon must have been a very grand place indeed. Even today, it is still a place which every visitor to Athens should see twice: once by day when, upon close inspection, the apparently white sunlit marble columns prove to have developed a warm, honey-coloured glow over the years; and again by night, when the ruins are bathed in floodlighting as they feature as in a dramatic 'son et lumière' presentation relating their history. In the summer there is nightly 'son et lumière' in English, except during the full moon period when the heavens throw their own dramatic light on the ruins, and it really is one of the "musts" of any Grecian holiday–there is seating on the Hill of the Pnyx, opposite the Acropolis, and the presentation takes place to the accompaniment of countless flashes from amateur photographers who fondly imagine that modern electronic flash equipment is effective over a distance of half a mile.

It is impossible to miss the second great building on the 200-feet high Rock of the Acropolis, for the Propylaea, the imposing entrance to the Acropolis, is still the spot at which tours of the rock start. Boulders are strewn around the central gateway and its two wings, one of which was used by the ancients as a picture gallery. Both the Propylaea and the Parthenon are currently the subject of concern because of the damage caused by hundreds of thousands of visitors every year as well as by industrial chemicals in the air of Athens–yet the beauty of these buildings can only be properly appreciated by a visit to the rock, and as tourism increases so will the numbers of visitors to the Acropolis, which is one of the modern 'Wonders of the World'.

Damage to the rock is nothing new. It is still possible to see the marks of chariot wheels in the Propylaea. To the right of the the grand entrance is the delicate Temple of Athena Nike, also

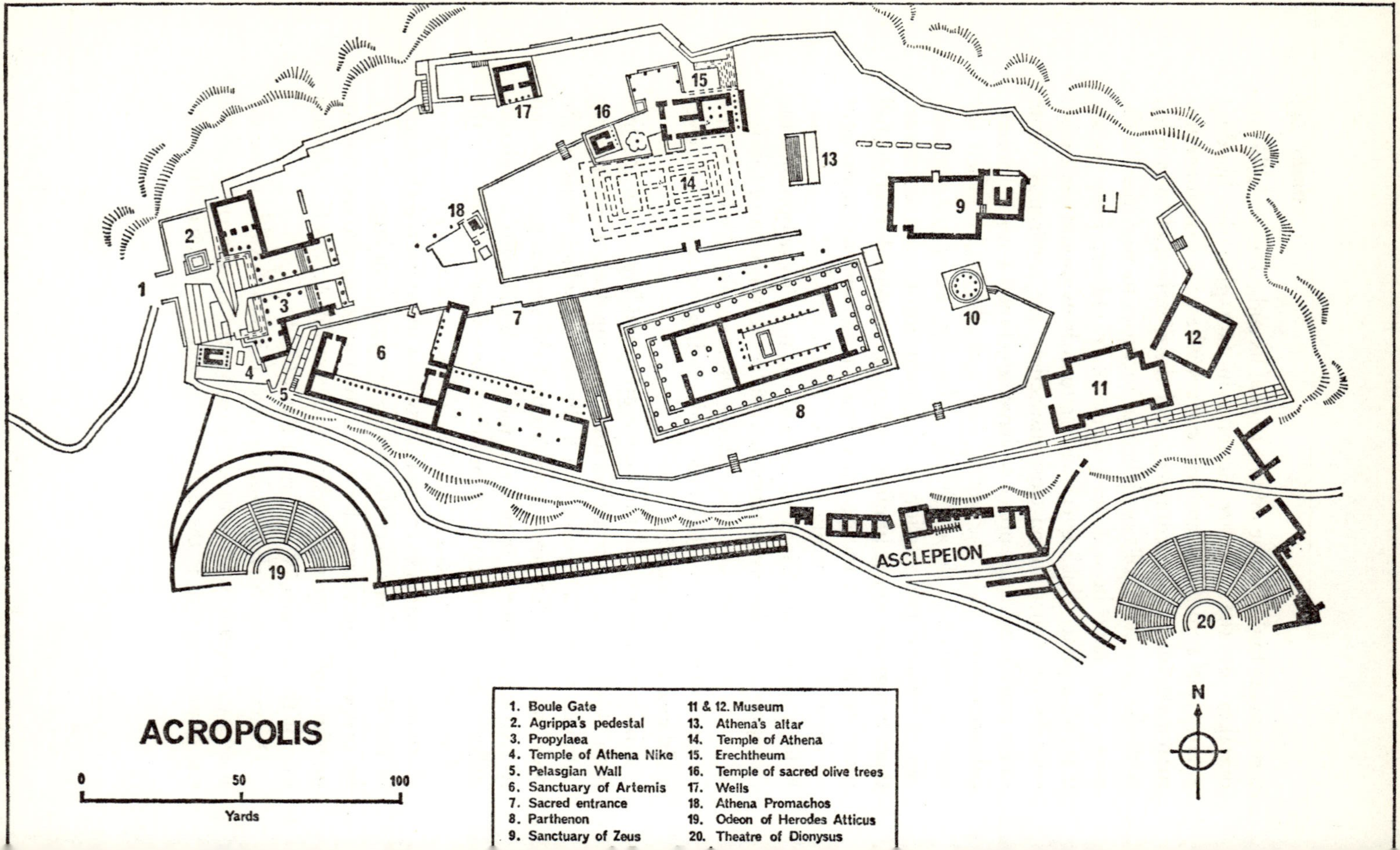

ACROPOLIS

1. Boule Gate
2. Agrippa's pedestal
3. Propylaea
4. Temple of Athena Nike
5. Pelasgian Wall
6. Sanctuary of Artemis
7. Sacred entrance
8. Parthenon
9. Sanctuary of Zeus
11 & 12. Museum
13. Athena's altar
14. Temple of Athena
15. Erechtheum
16. Temple of sacred olive trees
17. Wells
18. Athena Promachos
19. Odeon of Herodes Atticus
20. Theatre of Dionysus

known as 'Wingless Victory'. It was built to commemorate Greek victories over the Persians in the fifth century B.C., and its frieze depicts scenes from the battles. Finally, to the north of the Parthenon, is the Erechtheum, an elegant Ionic temple built on several levels and incorporating the monumental porch supported by the six caryatids—columns in the shape of women. If the Parthenon suffered the abuse of being used as a powder magazine during the Turkish occupation, the Erechtheum suffered an even greater indignity: it was used to house the Turkish governor's harem.

The Acropolis is a place to linger, despite the suffocating heat there in midsummer when the sunlight reflects blindingly off the stones. There are magnificent views across the rooftops of Athens to the glittering waters of the Saronic Gulf, or towards Mount Hymettus and the other hills on either side of Athens, which spread a famous violet light across the plain a little before sunset. There is an excellent and cunningly-concealed museum on the rock, and at the foot of the Acropolis are two antique theatres: the ruined Theatre of Dionysus, where Athenians once gathered to watch day-long Greek tragedies during the Festival of the Dionysia; and the Theatre of Herodus Atticus, a comparatively modern edifice which used to be roofed and dates only from the second century, which is the setting for the modern Athens Festival of Music and Drama held every summer.

Beyond the Acropolis are smaller hills which are also rich in history—the rocky Aeropagus, where St Paul delivered his sermons to the Athenians, and the Pnyx which, long before it was taken over as seating for the 'son et lumière' performances, was the meeting place of the General Assembly of ancient Athens.

Beside these memorials to 'the glory that was Greece', the other archaeological splendours of Athens fade into comparative insignificance. Hadrian's octagonal clocktower (the 'Tower of the Winds'), the gigantic yet graceful columns of the Olympeion (the 'Temple of Olympian Zeus'), the well-preserved Theseion temple with its frieze depicting the exploits of Theseus and

Heracles, and Hadrian's Arch are scarcely spared more than a glance by any except travellers with specialist archaeological knowledge or interests. Yet all are worth a closer look and, to my mind anyway, all are steeped in atmosphere.

Below the Rock of the Acropolis lies the old Athens, the Plaka. Here, in the maze of narrow streets, are the best shopping bargains: jewellery, sponges, leather goods, handicrafts, pottery, and ironwork. Here 'Melissinos the Poet' will produce made-to-measure sandals for you while you wait, even if you don't appreciate his poetry, and around the corner, over sticky coffee brought in by a boy swinging a long-handled tray from his hands, a young English couple with a shop devoted to folk art will help you to pore over the trays of 'evil eye' charms—the blue stones dotted with white and black, like an eye, which the superstitious Greeks solemnly assure you will ward off evil.

And here, at night, the whitewashed rooftop restaurants throb as *bouzouki* players—or, more correctly, exponents of that appalling and far-from-traditional intrument, the electronic *bouzouki*—vie with each other to see who can play the latest pop tunes the loudest.

It may sound awful, but somehow it isn't. The Plaka seems to come alive at night: it is a place to walk, to meet friends, to talk, to dance, or just feel happy. Even if you have been in Athens for only half a day, you may find acquaintances in the Plaka. One evening I was greeted as an old friend by a shopkeeper whose premises I had visited for the first time only a few hours before, and which I had left without buying anything. 'Come', he cried. 'It is marvellous to meet again. We must have a drink together.' His look became crafty as he added, conspiratorially: 'But you must not tell my wife that I was here.'

A few yards farther on I met the Athenian travel agent who had arranged part of my trip and was promptly invited to join him and his wife for dinner in one of the rooftop restaurants, decorated with a green wooden trellis and half-smothered in hibiscus and bougainvillea. The Greeks have their personal favourites among these restaurants and *tavernas* in the Plaka, but there is no accurate guide to them; you just have to trust to luck or to the advice of a friend or of a passer-by. But the traditional appetiser of *ouzo* will calm any fears; you will be quickly caught up in the gaiety of the atmosphere even if you are dining alone, and in most restaurants there are no menu difficulties—for you choose your main dish simply by walking into the kitchen and pointing.

And next morning, there is still a great deal to see. To cure a hangover, climb to the top of Mount Lycabettus—up a steep and winding road through wooded parkland, with the now familiar panorama of Athens unfolding below you, until you reach the little whitewashed Byzantine Chapel of St George at the top. There is also a small restaurant at the summit, and the sort of view—particularly across to the Acropolis—that one might expect from a vantage point more than 900 feet high. At Easter there is a spectacular candlelight procession on Mount Lycabettus, with hundreds of people carrying candles zig-zagging their way down the path from the top and turning the hill into one of Athens' most beautiful sights. A more prosaic descent for tourists is by the funicular railway, which can also be used on the way up if you really need it. The train quickly deposits you back in the bustle of the streets at the foot of the hill.

Perhaps surprisingly, in view of the city's history, the churches of Athens lack both variety and interest—although the three Byzantine churches are gems of their kind. The Byzantine-style Cathedral of Athens (in fact a nineteenth-century construction) dwarfs the tiny Church of Aghios Eleftherios, built of marble during the thirteenth century, beside it. There are small twelfth-century brick churches at the corner of Klafthmonos Square (Aghii Theodori) and in Ermou Street (the Church of Kapnikarea), but both have been surrounded by modern buildings, without regard for either good taste or for history. The other apparently Byzantine churches scattered around Athens are all later copies.

With its penchant for mixing past and present, it is perhaps not surprising that in providing the setting for the 1896 Olympic

Games, Athens chose to build, on a central site, an accurate replica of an ancient Roman stadium which can nevertheless seat 70,000 spectators in modern comfort. The white marble stadium is a surprisingly attractive structure, but the rock tunnel at the end of the arena has a bloody history—for it was an exit tunnel used during shows involving wild animals which were put on in the original stadium on this site in Roman times.

Between the Stadium and Syntagma are two large parks which comprise a welcome oasis in the heart of Athens. Beside Parliament House, and running down to the roundabout where traffic sweeps round Hadrian's Arch, is the frontage of the informally-landscaped Royal Gardens, its shady paths bordered by carefully-tended shrubs and flowers. Beyond the Royal Gardens are the less attractive Zapion Gardens, which surround the Zapion exhibition halls.

The chief museum in Athens, and by far the most interesting, is the National Archaeological Museum in Patission Avenue, near Omonia. Every period of ancient Greek civilisation is covered by the exhibits, with finds from excavations throughout the country. The Mycenaean collection is probably the highlight, with the exquisite work on the gold dishes, ornaments, and death masks found in the royal tombs at Mycenae throwing new light on the artistic abilities of Bronze Age craftsmen. Classical exhibits naturally abound, with pride of place going to some of the statues, such as the majestic bronze Zeus about to hurl one of his thunderbolts. The museum is closed on Mondays.

In the same building the Numismatic Museum houses no less than 250,000 ancient coins, while there is a collection of valuable historical inscriptions in the adjoining Epigraphical Museum.

Other museums worth visiting are the Museum of Greek Handicrafts in Aeros Street; the Benaki Museum in Coumbari Street for its icons; and the National Historical Museum in Stadiou Street, which deals with Greek history from 1821 up to the present. The Byzantine Museum, at 22 Vasilissis Sophias Avenue, is housed in an attractive nineteenth-century house and gives the tourist who is going on to one or more of the principal Byzantine sites outsdie Athens a foretaste of delights to come, for it contains outstanding examples of Byzantine, post-Byzantine, and old Christian art in the shape of temple decorations, jewellery, sculpture, icons, and copies of wall mosaics.

Although excursions from Athens are dealt with in Chapter 4, one cannot leave the city without considering the port area, Piraeus, and the beginning of the ribbon development along the coast of the Saronic Gulf, south of the city, towards Cape Sounion. Both areas are part of what might be described as 'Greater Athens'.

Piraeus, immortalised in the film *Never on a Sunday*, is a crowded and busy port, which always seems to be crammed with cruise liners as well as with the numerous island ferries which start their trips there and the other assorted shipping associated with any Mediterranean port. It is, in fact, one of the busiest harbours in the Mediterranean, and as the film suggested its waterfront houses a busy nightlife too—although the entertainments are of a somewhat down-to-earth nature and frequently arouse the interest of the city's police force. The adjacent port of Zea, with its yacht marina, is more attractive, while 'the little harbourside *taverna*' that your friends have told you about was probably not in Piraeus or Zea at all, but in the almost circular Turkolimano, or 'Turkish harbour', a pretty spot which is ringed with small restaurants and bars decorated with multi-coloured awnings and specialising in fresh fish. Turkolimano is a popular spot with Greek diners on a summer evening, and is easily reached by taxi or by catching the Omonia-Piraeus underground railway and getting off at Neon Faleron.

The tentacles of Athens now stretch for 16 miles down the Apollo Coast—or 'the Athens Riviera', as the inclusive tour companies using hotels there prefer to call it—to the headland at Vouliagmeni where what is undoubtedly the area's best hotel, the 'Luxury' graded Astir Palace, has been built. Between the city and Vouliagmeni are a string of resorts: Phaleron and Kalamaki, with their nightclubs and restaurants, Glyfada, Voula, Kavouri, and a smattering of smaller places. This area as much beloved by tour operators, principally because of the desperate shortage of hotel accommodation in the city itself, and some brochures go so far as to describe establishments in places like Glyfada as 'your Athens hotel'. It is an important point to bear in mind, because there are several major drawbacks to this coast. Many of the hotels are very basic; the beaches are cleaned frequently, but the same cannot be said for the sea which appears to be heavily polluted; Athens airport is situated along the coast, so there is a continual barrage of noise from low-flying jets; and the coast itself is a popular mooring for very large naval vessels. Athens is a city which people either love or hate—and in my experience the people who profess to hate it have usually stayed not in Athens, but somewhere along the sadly misnamed 'Riviera'.

Eating out and shopping in the Greek capital are dealt with in more detail in the following chapter. As far as hotels are concerned, the high demand for accommodation in or near the central areas means that it is essential to book in advance. Of the top-grade hotels, the Grande Bretagne in Constitution Square (with its long-established popularity among British guests), the Acropole Palace, and the Athens Hilton are probably the nicest—although changing standards, and the impossibility of personally trying out every major hotel, make recommendations in a city the size of Athens rather iniquitous. The King Minos is a good 'A' grade hotel, while I will be eternally grateful to the centrally-situated but unassuming 'B' grade Pan Hotel for once helping me out over a very tight spot concerning emergency accommodation at the height of the summer season.

This chapter will finish where it began—at Daphni. All too often, the Monastery of Daphni is lumped together with a tour of the classical sites in the Peloponnese peninsula, for as has already been indicated it is conveniently situated on the main road out to Corinth and the west. But the monastery, protected by high battlements, is worthy of a visit on its own because the eleventh-century church contains a superb collection of Byzantine mosaics, including the dramatic mosaic of Christ Pantocrator in the dome which is probably one of the best examples of its kind in the country, as well as being a formidable and awe-inspiring work of art.

Less happily, Daphni is the site of an annual wine festival, held every summer, when the country's wine-growers exhibit their wares in a wooded grove and men and women in national costume serve visitors with as many 'samples' as they like from the contents of a choice of 90 barrels. Greed has turned what should have been a charming festival into a bunfight, and the setting is particularly inapposite. The city's most convenient camping site is also situated at Daphni, in a spacious and sheltered glade which is unfortunately infested with mosquitos.

3. Eating, Drinking and Shopping

A few years ago it was common to read and hear quite savage attacks on the awfulness of Greek food, with travel experts advising holidaymakers to carry with them every medicament imaginable short of a stomach pump. It is doubtful whether these criticisms were ever justified, but they are certainly not true today. Admittedly many Greek dishes are an acquired taste, and admittedly the only *taverna* to be found in some very remote parts may be—to say the least—somewhat basic. A diet of stale, oily meat and *retsina*, the resinated wine so beloved by Greeks, will play havoc with the hardiest constitution; but no doubt a Greek would be equally upset by an elderly pork pie and some greasy tea in a grubby roadside cafe in England. Eat wisely in Greece, and you will eat well. Indeed, a meal will quickly become the prolonged pleasure that it is to almost every Greek.

The first secret of any Greek meal is not to be in a rush—because even if you are, the waiters won't be. Office hours in Greece are broken by a long siesta in the afternoon, so even a light lunch need not be a hurried affair. Businessmen work late, then join their friends or family for what is often the social highlight of the day: dinner. And whether they are eating at home, or in a restaurant or *taverna*, the Greeks like to sit long over their aperitifs

5 *The Corinth Canal*

IC
XC

(usually aniseed-flavoured *ouzo*, which turns cloudy when you add water or ice and is surprisingly strong), and then chat between courses. The men may even stand up, and perform a lonely *syrtaki* dance, when the mood takes them—it is bad manners to applaud such dancing, but tourists usually clap and will be forgiven for their ignorance.

At a party, or feast, the usual system is for the waiters to bring course after course to the table and for people to take whatever they want; at such meals appetites are always exhausted long before the menu is. In some very remote areas the old Eastern European and Middle Eastern custom of eating from a communal pot still survives, although tourists are unlikely to come across this. What holidaymakers may find when eating with Greeks, however, is that they are offered a choice piece of meat, or fruit, from their companion's plate in the middle of the meal—a complimentary gesture which should not be refused. Equally, it is dangerous to slip into the childish habit of leaving 'the best bit' on your own plate until last—for your neighbour may well reach across and help himself!

But these idiosyncracies are rare in towns like Athens. All you have to contend with there is a menu which may be totally unintelligible.

This is no problem in the smaller *tavernas*, where customers act as they still do in country areas and walk into the kitchen to choose the main course. Nobody will be surprised by such an action in Greece, and the state of the kitchen will do much to ease any remainining qualms that you may have about Greek food, for every *taverna* kitchen that I have ever seen has been spotless, even if it was cramped, hot, and overcrowded.

If you want to be adventurous with your choice of food, then a peep into the kitchen will certainly aid your choice. But if not —what should you choose?

6 Daphni: the dome of the Byzantine church

Two very safe choices are *souvlaki*, which is meat, usually lamb, grilled on a spit, and *moussaka*, a delicious pie containing minced meat and eggplant. Both are always made with fresh meat. A side salad, or *salata*, is usually ordered too, and this is a delicious affair sprinkled with olives as well as the more usual salad ingredients. Before the main course there are snacks known as *mezethes*, or very tasty *taramosalata*, a creamy paste made of fish roes and often eaten with hot bread.

In a country which lives so close to the sea, fish dishes are naturally common. Tiny red mullet (*barbounia*), grilled and eaten whole, are a tasty speciality, and sea bream (*lithinria*) are good too. Visitors should also ensure that they do not leave the country without tasting *kalamarakia*—crisply fried pieces of young squid. In the islands shellfish are popular, and a sort of *pilaff* is made of shrimps and prawns.

Other Greek favourites are *dolmathes* (stuffed vine leaves, served hot or cold), *avgolemono*, which is a lemon-flavoured chicken soup, and *youvarlakia* (boiled meat balls with rice). The hard *feta* goat cheese, found all over the country, can be recommended—and of course there is fruit to follow, although your Greek companions may well choose sticky sweets instead. Many places also make their own yoghourt, which connoisseurs always rate highly.

The water is good almost everywhere, and especially good in Athens, and there are also a number of local mineral waters. Beer is more expensive than wine and some brands are not very good; but you may need it after a day in the hot sun, and if that is the case Amstel is the best. With many areas producing their own wines, the choice can be bewildering in the best restaurants and non-existent in small country *tavernas*—but Greek wines are, as a general rule, pleasantly light. Of the non-resinated wines, Demestica, from the Peloponnese, and the fuller-bodied Naoussa red wine from Macedonia, are popular. Although some people take to *retsina*—wine flavoured with resin to help it travel—right away, others can never acquire the taste; but it is something to try and restaurateurs or *taverna* owners will be pleased to recommend a bottle without too much resin.

Although the various local wines—particularly those made in the islands, which are mentioned later in this book—are often very good, the same cannot always be said of the local brandies. Brandy drinkers should stick to Metaxa, although even that is rough compared with its Western European counterparts.

Apart from the food, perhaps the greatest attraction of Greek *tavernas*, as well as some restaurants, is that they are also places of entertainment. There may be a resident band, or singer, in popular spots like the Plaka in Athens, while in less sophisticated parts you may find simply a *bouzouki* player or even a waiter who every now and again stops serving at table and sings a song or two instead. And if there is no live entertainment, you may well find that the proprietor has made the best of a bad job and installed a jukebox. If that is the case—don't be put off; the records will all be Greek. Greek diners love a lot of noise.

Tavernas also have one other great factor in their favour: they will never turn you away. Once, when I stopped at a *taverna* in a quiet corner of Rhodes for a drink and decided to stay for an early lunch, the whole family got to work. The proprietor set the table and poured *ouzo*, his wife grilled fish, and a diminutive child was sent running for bread and *feta* cheese. If I had realised that I was, by Greek standards, too early for a meal I would never have put them to the inconvenience, but they would not hear of my leaving and insisted upon providing more drinks while I waited. The final bill: just a few pence. A similar thing happened in Corfu, where the owner of an attractive little taverna, learning that I was staying alone nearby, had my breakfast waiting for me every morning at a table set out under the vines. His only regret was that he could not persuade me to drink the thick Greek coffee, served in tiny cups which seem half full of sediment. Fellow-sufferers will be glad to learn that Nescafé is available all over Greece.

The Greek sweet tooth does have one material benefit for

tourists, in that it has led to the establishment of the admirable Floca cake shops, of which there are several in Athens. They also sell good chocolates, which they will gift-wrap for you. Perhaps even better is Loubier's, in Leoforos Kifissios. An ice-cream is a popular midday refreshment in the capital, but instead of joining the crowds and paying the earth in Constitution Square, go to quiet Kolonaki Square, just around the corner, where the pavement cafes are less crowded and the ices rather better. Off Kolonaki Square, in Scoufa Street, one baker specialises in hot croissants–ideal for a picnic lunch. Two fairly centrally-situated *taverna*-type restaurants worth remembering are Costoyannis's, in Zaimi Road, Alexandros Avenue, and Tria Adelfia, in Platia Victoria, which both serve good but inexpensive meals.

Shopping for souvenirs in Greece is an adventure. There are some excellent bargains to be found, but both quality and prices vary sharply from place to place. Many visitors to Athens head first for the Flea Market at the end of Ifestou, with its curious mixture of genuine-looking antiques and straightforward rubbish; but if they think they are going to find a genuine Byzantine icon at a knockdown price, they can forget it. Quite apart from the fact that exporting antiquities without a licence is forbidden, the Greeks have developed the faking of 'antiques' into an art.

If you are going on to the islands, handicrafts and other locally produced goods–sponges, for example–are likely to be cheaper there. Corfu and the Ionian Islands, and Rhodes, are the best places for jewellery, while the Ionian Islands and the Cyclades also have the biggest (and cheapest) selection of embroidered clothing. Remember, too, that you can bargain in the islands–a practice which Athenian shopkeepers turn their noses up at nowadays.

Furs, from the northern town of Kastoria, are one of the best buys in Greece, and in Athens the furriers Sistovaris have four shops, including one in the Hilton Hotel. Shoes–in leather, of course–are also very good value, and besides the sandals that are made up for passers-by in the Plaka area, women can have more formal shoes made to measure at Kozatsa's, in Kanari Street just off Kolonaki Square.

Nikis Street, parallel to Constitution Square behind the American Express building, has a number of boutiques and a couple of cut-price shops selling cheap shampoos and other toiletries. The Ambelokopi area also has several boutiques, with a good choice of clothes for women, but up-to-date menswear is not worth buying because it is usually imported and is therefore expensive. Shops deserving special mention are Prisunic, a sort of cross between Marks and Spencer and Woolworth, which has cheap clothes as well as selling food, and the huge shoeshop called simply Shoes, in Harilaou Trikoupi Street, where there is a big choice of comfortable leather shoes at reasonable prices. All the major shops in Athens have two sales a year—from 1 to 20 February and from 1 to 20 August.

Souvenir ideas include woven and leather bags, other leather goods of all kinds, peasant-type blouses, lamps (Athens has a big selection, and they are cheap), pottery, brasswork, and coloured braid for dresses or other items of clothing. And, finally, nobody goes home without at least one set of *kombolia*, the brightly-coloured worry beads with which Greeks play interminably.

4. Excursions from Athens

Athens lies within easy reach of many of the most popular tourist spots in Greece, and there is a rich and varied choice of excursions from the capital—by car, by coach, by train, or by boat.

Several of these places are mentioned in their own right elsewhere in this book: Daphni and the Apollo Coast were dealt with in Chapter 2, and the old city-states of the Peloponnese—such as Mycenae, Sparta, and Corinth—are mentioned in detail in the next chapter, as are Olympia and Epidaurus. The daily ferry services from Piraeus also put the Cyclades, and even the Dodecanese Islands and Crete, within comparatively easy reach, and these are all discussed in the chapters under the relevant subject headings.

One of the problems about making any sort of excursion from Athens in the summer is that the heat can really sap one's energy to an extent that I have not experienced in any other European city. Given the choice between an afternoon's drive to Cape Sounion or a *siesta*, there is a very real danger that visitors of every age will follow the example of the Athenians themselves and settle for the *siesta*.

Don't—because Cape Sounion really is worth seeing, especially if you can time it so that you are there at sunset. The Cape, a perpendicular cliff rising sheer from the sea, is crowned by the fifth-century-B.C. Temple of Poseidon, with twelve Doric columns remaining erect. The visiting Byron carved his name on one of the slender white columns, and because the headland juts out into the Aegean at the mouth of the Saronic Gulf, the pillars are also the first—and last—glimpse which sea travellers catch of mainland Greece. From the Temple of Poseidon can be seen a panorama of sea and islands, and the view is particularly spectacular at sunset when the temple assumes a rosy mantle which generations of Greeks and tourists alike have found very romantic.

The trip to Cape Sounion, 53 miles from the centre of Athens, is often combined with a drive back through the Mesogea, or midlands, an area dotted with tiny villages and some good *tavernas* where Athenians like to go to eat in an open-air setting surrounded by sweet-smelling flowers and shrubs. A branch road leads off to Marathon and the site of the famous Athenian victory over the Persians.

The people of Athens like to escape from the city's heat during the summer, and evening drives to the beach, or up into the cooler hill resorts nearby, are popular. Suburban Kifissia is especially nice—you can get there on a number 25 bus from Athens, then hire a horse-drawn carriage for a ride up the slopes of Mount Pentele, which provided most of the marble used in building the temples of the Acropolis. There are pleasant *cafenions* in Politea (bus 18a from Athens), and at Kaisariani, on the flowery slopes of Mount Hymettus, there is the double attraction of a Byzantine monastery with fine frescoes as well as extensive views of Athens far below. Mount Parnes, the highest of the three mountains which rise above the capital, is a popular summer resort as well as a winter sports centre, and there is a casino in the Hotel Mont-Parnes.

Island lovers will not want to miss the two groups of islands which are the easiest to reach from Athens: the five islands in the Saronic Gulf, opposite the capital, and—farther away to the east—the sprawling but increasingly popular islands of the Sporades group.

Of the Saronic Gulf islands, all but Salamis and Aegina seem to belong geographically to the Peloponnese, and are dealt with in the next chapter. But Salamis is interesting in its proximity to the mainland (it is just a 20-minute ferry ride from Piraeus), while Aegina, only 16 miles offshore, is perhaps the first place where one can find the restful and even timeless air which is associated with the Cyclades Islands to the south-east.

The seven-mile strait which separates Salamis from the mainland is the site of the sea battle in which the Athenians destroyed the Persian fleet in 480 B.C. Today those same waters are criss-crossed by modern ferries, many of them heading for Paloukia, the island's main port. There is a good road to the island's capital, Koulouri, a couple of miles away, which is in fact no more than a quiet fishing port with good restaurants and *tavernas* specialising in shellfish and seafood. From Koulouri the road winds through olive groves and fields of vegetables, then climbs pine-covered hills to the Convent of Faneromeni, where a horrific mural of the last judgment depicts more than 3,000 damned and tortured figures.

Aegina, more or less at the centre of the Saronic Gulf, draws most of its tourists from among visiting yachtsmen. The island's rich soil makes it farming country, but besides dairy products it produces pistacchio nuts and juicy figs. The main town, after which the island is named, is a pretty spot, with narrow streets and alleys lined by blue-domed churches and pink and white classical-style houses. Open-air cafés and restaurants line the waterfront.

About eight miles outside the town (an easy bus journey) is the Doric Temple of Aphaia, the most visited site on the island and built in a splendid setting. Along with the solitary fluted column still standing in the town, which is all that remains of ancient Aegina, the temple is a reminder that Aegina was once an important city-state in its own right with a powerful fleet—too powerful, in fact, for the Athenians, who could not accept what they spitefully described as 'the eyesore of Piraeus' as such a neighbour. Athens conquered Aegina in 454 B.C., and after that the island declined—although it enjoyed a brief return to former glory in 1828 when, for a period of just under nine months, it was the official Greek capital.

The fishing village of Aghia Marina, a sandy bay backed by pine-clad hills, with good *tavernas*, and hotel and bungalow developments on either side of the bay, is a good place to stay on Aegina. The medieval and Byzantine capital of Palaeochora, clinging to a rock as a protection against pirate attacks, is worth visiting, and there are alkali and radium springs at Souvala said to be good for arthritic conditions, rheumatism and eczema.

Those other islands in the Athens area, the Sporades, are in fact a half-hour flight to the north of the city, with car ferry connections to Evia and Lamia. If they seem out of place in a chapter about excursions from the capital, one can only point out that it is via Athens that most visitors arrive, and that the islands seem even more out of place linked to any other part of mainland Greece. For the four islands—Skiathos, Skopelos, Alonnissos, and Skyros—have a languid atmosphere all of their own, a fact which has undoubtedly contributed to their growing popularity both as holiday destinations and as excursion spots.

But it is possible to have reservations about the Sporades. The people do not seem as friendly as elsewhere in Greece, and transport both to the islands and within the group leaves a lot to be desired.

Skiathos is the best-known of the Sporades—a soft, green island, with lovely beaches and an increasingly sophisticated tourist industry. The principal town, also called Skiathos, contains several hotels along its cobbled streets, and from it the island's only stretch of road travels the six miles to the famous beach at Koukounares, via the Kalamaki peninsula where there has been considerable villa development. To get to the island's other beaches—70 of them altogether—you either walk or hire a boat. The pebbled beach at Lalaria, with its crystal-clear water, is one of the best, and Krassa and Aghia Eleni also have their advocates. The undeveloped north coast of the island is harsher, and the sea often seems rougher.

There are two 'A'-grade hotels on Skiathos, and the Skiathos

Palace, at Koukounares, is recommended. There are a handful of cheaper hotels, but you can rent a room in the town of Skiathos very cheaply indeed. Many of the beach *tavernas* are excellent; *moussaka* is a local speciality, but several have also adopted the admirable practice of cooking anything a customer requires as long as they are given advance notice. Perhaps the biggest problem on Skiathos is that the buses stop running at 8 p.m., so evenings out have a distinctly local flavour.

Where Skiathos leads, can Skopelos be far behind? The answer, surprisingly, is yes—for although Skopelos is a very beautiful island indeed, with fine beaches, a colourful town, and women who still wear the picturesque native costume of embroidered silk skirt, short velvet coat with flowing sleeves, and a fine silk headscarf, the tourist invasion has not yet arrived there. But there is a strong tradition of hospitality, and the charm and interest of Skopelos undoubtedly mark it down as an island which is about to be 'discovered'. The people of Skopelos have a charming custom in which they present departing visitors with a sprig of sweet basil or a gardenia, meaning 'Please come again'. It is an invitation which many people are going to accept.

It is less easy to be kind about Alonissos and Skyros. Alonissos is a humid, oblong-shaped island, given over to farming and fishing, and the islanders give every appearance of disliking visitors—an attitude which one rarely comes across in Greece. Rocky Skyros, which is harder to reach than the other islands, is strictly for people who do not mind 'roughing it', although the folk art shops have a tempting range of hand-carved furniture.

In complete contrast to the islands, one of the best-known and most popular excursions from Athens is to Delphi, perched between earth and sky on the foothills of Mount Parnassus and in ancient times the holiest place in Greece.

Ideally this is a two-day trip, for Delphi is more than 100 miles from Athens. But even if time is short, the excursion should not be missed, and the spot which was once known as 'the navel of Greece' holds a key to the country even today. The place has an extraordinary atmosphere, and if there is time to soak it up then that is all the better for in that way it is easier to understand that Delphi is more than ruins, legends and history.

No doubt the dramatic setting first drew men's attention to the site. The road from Levadia, the old Sacred Way, climbs high into the mountains, past the precipitous mountain village of Arahova, and almost to the 8,000-feet summit of Mount Parnassus before dropping down towards Delphi—a spot almost as emotive as one's first glimpse of the Acropolis. There is a lively modern village, full of souvenir shops, and from the main road there are splendid views over the sheer valley below. From the entrance to the site, the Sacred Way zig-zags down to the Temple of Apollo. It was through the cult of Apollo that Delphi grew in importance —but it was internationally famous as the seat of the oracle whose advice political and military leaders from all over the Mediterranean eagerly sought between the eighth century and the fourth century B.C., and for which they paid liberally. Delphi became rich, and one passes several ruined treasuries, and the reconstructed Treasury of the Athenians, on the way to the Temple of Apollo. Inscribed in the marble of the Treasury is a sentence dedicating to Apollo the Athenian spoils from the Battle of Marathon.

Not much remains of the Temple of Apollo, the centre of the shrine which held sway over so much of the known world for 600 years. The podium and peristyle are complete, and some Doric columns have been erected in their original position, and this is enough to give an idea of the layout of the sanctuary, and of the spot where the oracle—always an elderly woman who had undergone a complex 'purification' ceremony—sat over a fissure in the rock (later sealed by earth tremors) and breathed in subterranean fumes while working herself into a trance. It is now thought that the fumes may have been carbon monoxide, which would account for the fact that many of the oracle's 'prophecies' were totally unintelligible. But the days on which the oracle, speaking 'with the voice of Apollo', pronounced (always in February, which was Apollo's birth month) were eagerly awaited,

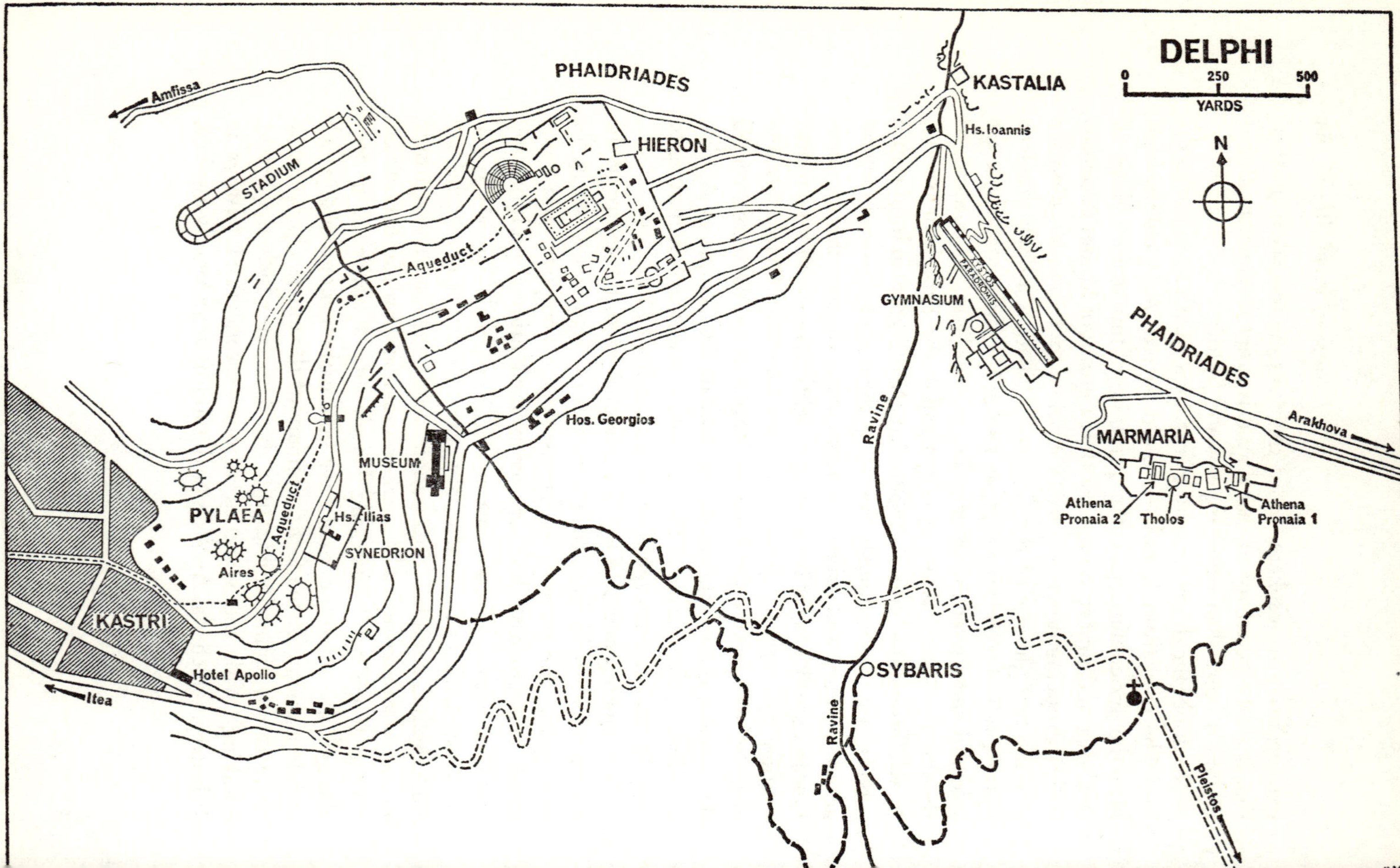
DELPHI
0
250
500
YARDS
N
PHAIDRIADES
KASTALIA
Hs. Ioannis
Amfissa
STADIUM
HIERON
Aqueduct
GYMNASIUM
XYSTOS
PARADROMIS
PHAIDRIADES
Arakhova
MARMARIA
Athena
Pronaia 2
Tholos
Athena
Pronaia 1
Ravine
Hos. Georgios
MUSEUM
Hs. Ilias
SYNEDRION
PYLAEA
Aqueduct
Aires
KASTRI
Hotel Apollo
Itea
SYBARIS
Ravine
Pleistos

and in return for money or other riches she would pronounce on anything from affairs of state to affairs of the heart. The oracle's ramblings and frequent failures led to scepticism, of course—although the people of Delphi discouraged sacrilege by making it punishable by death. She improved her tarnished image by predicting the future of Athens as a naval power (saying that the city would be saved by its 'wooden walls') as well as forecasting the defeat, in the snow, of a Gallic attack on Delphi itself (with an enigmatic reference to 'the white maidens'). But the greed of the Emperor Nero who looted the site, an earthquake, and the coming of Christianity, combined to bring about the eventual decay of Delphi.

The group of ruins known as the Marmaria, as well as the gymnasium, the stadium, and the theatre—originally built to seat 5,000, and still used occasionally for performances of Greek tragedy—should be seen. And visitors cannot miss the museum, on the road between the village and the site; it contains some fine examples of early Greek sculpture, including a fifth-century-B.C. bronze of a charioteer which is believed to have been placed on a wall above the Temple of Apollo, and the impressive Winged Sphinx of the Naxians.

Trips to Delphi are often combined with a visit to the Monastery of Osias Loukas, an important Byzantine monument in the hills above the main road to Levadia. Named after a tenth-century saint and prophet, the monastery has two interconnecting churches, the larger one containing superb eleventh-century mosaics which took more than 100 years to complete and are even bigger and more intricate than those at Daphni. There is a particularly spectacular Nativity, and the church—whose architectural form of an octagon roofed with a dome served as a model for many subsequent Byzantine churches—has large windows and numerous galleries and niches which create an impression of size despite its small proportions. The wall paintings in the crypt date from the eleventh century and are also significant.

5. The Peloponnese

Strictly speaking the Peloponnese peninsula, which forms the southern part of the Greek mainland, is now an island. Hanging into the Mediterranean like a vast mulberry leaf, 'Pelops' Isle' is separated from the rest of the country by the Gulf of Corinth. A strip of land less than four miles wide links the Peloponnese to the mainland, and as early as the seventh-century-B.C. Greek sailors and statesmen dreamed of cutting a canal through the rock. The Romans were particularly aware of the strategic and commercial advantages which would result from linking the Gulf of Corinth and the Saronic Gulf—Caesar, Caligula, and Hadrian studied the idea closely, and Nero actually dug the first traces of a canal with a golden spade. But the rock proved too tough, and big ships had to continue making the long journey round Cape Tainaron, the southernmost tip of the Peloponnese, while smaller vessels were often lifted on to huge sledges and dragged overland across the isthmus. Traces of the Diolkos, the stone track used by the sledges, can still be found.

British dynamite finally completed the achievement which Nero and Caesar had dreamed of, and the Corinth Canal—6,939 yards long but only 75 feet wide—was completed in 1893. As the sea washed through the gash in the rocks, the Poleponnese became the largest of the Greek islands.

But, of course, it is still treated as part of the mainland—albeit as a region with distinct characteristics of its own. And the Corinth Canal became one of the most popular of the area's tourist attractions. Although cruise liners are usually too big to pass through the canal, it is used by many smaller ferries on which people often travel simply to make the brief but dramatic passage. The sheer rock walls soar high above the ship, and seem almost to shut out the sky.

With Patras, Corinth is probably the most visited city in the Peloponnese, and both are linked with Athens by a fast motorway. Today Corinth is a modern city, conscious of its role as a communications crossroads and catering for the visitor with convenient shops and hotels. The road bridge across the canal affords another fine view of the waterway, with the sea far below and looking hardly wide enough for even a rowing boat—the bridge is a good vantage point for photographers.

But in fact modern Corinth is not the town which played such a large part in Greek history. The new town was rebuilt in 1858 and 1928 after earthquakes; ancient Corinth lies 10 miles away high on a hill overlooking both the Gulf of Corinth and the Saronic Gulf. Although the ancient city-state was destroyed by the Romans in 146 B.C., and remained uninhabited for a century, a new colony was founded there by Caesar in 44 B.C., and visitors can still see the temple of Apollo, with its rare, monolithic Doric columns, as well as the Peirene Fountain, the market place, theatre, a number of Roman buildings, and the spot from which St Paul delivered his sermons to the reluctant Corinthians. The Acrocorinth, towering above the ancient city, was originally the site of a temple to Aphrodite. It was replaced by an immense Byzantine fortress, to which the Crusaders, Venetians, and Turks all added extensions. The climb up to the Acrocorinth is worthwhile, for there are magnificent views; in perfect conditions it is said that the sharp-eyed can see as far as the Parthenon in Athens, approximately 50 miles away.

People visiting the Peloponnese can usually be divided into two categories: those making an excursion from Athens to see the classical sites of Mycenae, Olympia, and Epidaurus with its famous theatre; and those who arrive in Greece on the ferries which terminate at Patras, which is in the north-west corner of the peninsula and is, after Piraeus and Thessalonika, the third port of Greece. But tourists hurrying west simply in search of antiquities, or heading east on their way to Athens, are missing some of the wildest and most magnificent scenery in Greece. For the Peloponnese is a peninsula in which one could quite happily spend many weeks just exploring the mountain villages, and visiting (especially on the south-west coast) what are probably the last totally unspoilt and almost deserted beaches in Europe.

Perhaps I like Patras because it is, quite literally, the first Greek town that I ever set eyes upon. 'Welcome to Greece' says a giant hoarding above the spot where the ferry boats from Italy dock, and the fact that the sign is written in English is perhaps the first indication of the sort of welcome that the newcomer to Greece can expect. Even the road signs, unintelligible to those with no knowledge of the Greek alphabet, have their legend repeated 50 yards along the road in Roman letters.

Many guidebooks dismiss Patras as merely a port whose architecture has been influenced, for better or worse, by past Venetian connections. But it is more than that. It is a pretty, open town, with shady arcaded streets, a Roman theatre, and a Frankish castle. It is also—despite the fact that St Andrew was crucified there—a friendly place, as I found some years ago when my British-made car developed a fault a few miles outside the town and 2,000 miles away from home. Greeks respond magnificently to such crises. Speaking no Greek, and surrounded by a growing number of 'guides' who spoke no English, I was led to a small back-street garage in Patras. My unscheduled arrival, which would have caused widespread gloom in any British garage, made the mechanics' day. Half a dozen heads disappeared beneath the bonnet; the shouting matches which pass for everyday Greek conversation grew more intense; and firm suntanned hands,

7 The Byzantine church of Osios Loukas

grasping a frightening array of hammers and spanners, got to work.

Watching Greek mechanics work on a car is rather like going to the doctor with a sore throat and being told to take all your clothes off; while they are at it, they mend everything in sight. Although my car was suffering only from a faulty fuel pump, the vehicle was jacked up, the wheels removed, the sparking plugs taken out, and people probed into everything from the radiator to the fuel tank. It worked, for the pump staged a miraculous recovery and, after effusive farewells, I was able to continue my journey.

Assistance is not always so informal. Like other principal cities on the Greek mainland, and like the holiday islands during the summer months, Patras has a force of Tourist Police—an admirable institution which other tourist-conscious countries would do well to copy. The duties of the Tourist Police are, quite simply, to help tourists; and the only thing wrong with the system is that too few people know about it.

Besides patrolling the streets, the Tourist Police operate from centrally-situated offices, and if asked they will find you anything from a parking place to a bed for the night. Their advice is usually excellent and their services should be remembered, for they are not mere tourist guides but have very real police powers which enable them to deal sharply and efficiently with any complaints about accommodation, service, or even the unwelcome and unreasoning attentions of the rest of the vast Greek bureaucratic machine. Put a Greek in uniform, and more often than not he quickly betrays an overbearing and officious attitude to which the only answer is *force majeure*. The Tourist Police represent such a force, and I was once very glad of the intercession of a Tourist Police officer in the docks at Piraeus to bring to a satisfactory conclusion an acrimonious discussion with a Greek customs

8 Mycenae: the Lion Gate

officer who was disputing the need for me, as a photographer, to carry more than one camera.

Because it is the port through which many 'do-it-yourself' holidaymakers enter Greece, Patras is infested with youths touting for hotels and camping sites. Ignore their advice, and the cards they press upon you. The Tourist Police and tourist authorities are in a far better position to advise about hotels, while in Greece the best camp sites are those run by the national motoring organisation, ELPA.

Almost uniquely in Europe, camping is permitted in Greece at almost any spot which takes the visitors' fancy, so the organised sites have to be both good and cheap. There is a good ELPA site at Rion, a few miles east of Patras, set in an olive grove, well equipped with washing and toilet facilities, and with its own little shingle beach lapped by the clear waters of the Gulf of Corinth. But, as a general rule, camp-site shopping facilities cannot be relied upon, while camp-site restaurants are best avoided.

All the way between Corinth and Patras, both the road and the railway follow the coastline overlooking the Gulf of Corinth. The scenery presents a contrast to the sunlit Saronic Gulf, for this area is dominated by the mountain ranges on the mainland to the north, which cast long shadows on to the water and create an atmosphere that often seems closer to that of the Italian lakes than to what one thinks of as 'typical' Greece.

From Patras, the most popular excursion is undoubtedly to Olympia, and the main road bypasses a number of pretty little seaside villages where visitors are still a rarity. In the 'spa' town of Kilini, from which the handsome new ferry *Proteus* makes three two-hour crossings a day to the nearby island of Zakinthos, the handful of houses along the big sandy beach feel that they are far enough away from the prying eyes of officialdom to overcharge casual visitors wanting to rent a room. Meals are much more reasonable, if only because the two nice harbourside restaurants are in direct competition with each other. And the mineral springs are said to be good for asthma, bronchitis, and skin complaints.

At Pyrgos, the road turns eastwards through the fertile green valley of Elis, one of the ancient city-states of the Peloponnese. And, at the junction of two rivers, at the foot of the pine-covered Mount Cronion, the Greeks unerringly chose to site one of their most important sanctuaries: Olympia. Here, from 776 B.C., in a temple dedicated to Zeus, the ancient Greeks forgot their quarrels for a period of truce every fourth year, and during this time athletes from the entire Hellenic world travelled to Olympia to compete in the Olympic Games. The Greeks themselves measured time from the games of 572 B.C., and the unity inherent in the athletics contests marked the beginning of the Hellenic ideal which has continued to this day. The area around Olympia became a centre for Greek art as the sanctuary was showered with gifts and offerings.

By 572 B.C. the Games, held between June and September, had become very important. Special messengers would set off in every direction to announce the beginning of a sacred truce and the suspension of all disputes and warfare between the various city-states. The contests lasted for five days each month, and included foot racing, wrestling, the pentathlon, chariot-racing, horse-racing, and artistic and literary competitions. The games were held regularly for a thousand years, and were not discontinued until shortly after the Roman conquest of Greece. Among the famous victors was the Emperor Nero, who took 'gold medals' in both chariot-racing and singing. Although anabolic steroids were unknown in those days Nero did, however, contrive to give himself certain advantages over his fellow-contestants: in the chariot racing he allowed himself ten horses while his rivals were allocated a maximum of six; and the singing contest that he won was both introduced and judged by himself.

The modern worldwide Olympic Games were introduced in 1896 by Baron de Coubertin, and—with a flame lit at ancient Olympia flickering over the contestants—they have been held at intervals of four years ever since, except during the First and Second World Wars.

Today, countries vie with each other to stage the Games. But no modern Olympics can hope to have as beautiful a setting as Olympia itself. Shaded and scented by the trees, it is an emotive spot where one can wander for hours among the stunted remains of the columns of the Altis, once the sanctuary of Zeus. An arched passage leads to the stadium, which can still be seen. There is also a fine museum nearby, containing the many archaeological finds made at the site—among them the pediments of the temple, and the famous statue of Hermes discovered near the ruins of Hera's Temple, on Cronion.

From Pyrgos, there is a good stretch of road—flattered by the Greeks with the title 'motorway'—leading down to another 'spa' village, Kaiafas (the natural springs are recommended for arthritic, gynaecological and skin complaints); Kiparissia, nestling under the ruins of a mediaeval castle; and the coastline opposite the erstwhile pirate hideout of Proti, an island which is still said to contain hoards of buried treasure. At Ano Eglianos, extensive excavations have been made on the site of an ancient palace where the clay tablets bearing the mysterious Linear-B script were discovered. A museum at Hora, close by, exhibits the precious tablets as well as other Mycenaean relics.

A few miles further south is Pylos, better known as Navarino, the site of two major Greek battles. Like neighbouring Methoni, it is an historical stronghold with Venetian fortifications. From Methoni there are ferries to the offshore islands of Sapientza and Schiza, and the area is also a spear-fishing centre. From Pylos the road branches north to the commercial centre of Kalamata, from which one can visit ancient Ithomi, and Sparta.

Ithomi was once a heavily fortified city which dominated the region, and it is worth climbing to the peak of Mount Ithomi with the remains of its ancient acropolis and an uninhabited monastery. Kalamata is a pleasant town, with good waterside restaurants and a string of Byzantine monasteries as well as a convent where the nuns still weave exquisite silks which are made into handkerchiefs and blouses. The drive to Sparta is a dramatic one, the road climbing to 3,300 feet at the Taygetos Pass before descending through the Langada Gorge with its view over a sea of olive trees on the plain of Sparta. Nothing remains of the collection of villages which made up ancient Sparta, but the modern town still manages to convey some of the austerity under which the ancient Spartans lived. Athens' ancient enemy was a military state, where young boys were whipped, and made to bathe in the icy river, as part of their training for manhood and a military career. Modern visitors, however, will not find accommodation spartan—there are several good hotels in the city.

Three miles west of Sparta, a pleasant walk through orange and lemon groves, are the ruins of the Frankish castle of Mistra, where a Byzantine town grew up beneath the protective walls. Turkish troops burned the town in 1770, but the remains—houses, palaces and churches—comprise a vast museum of Byzantine life. There are good late Byzantine wall paintings in several of the churches, particularly in Perivleptos. Mistra is an interesting and enchanting spot at any time, but is even more attractive when the *son et lumière* presentations during the 'Paleologia' pageant bring the city magically back to life.

Indeed, the whole of the southern Peloponnese is a happy hunting ground for the curious traveller. You can study more Byzantine churches—40 of them—in Monemvasia; wonder at the deserted towers of the Mani, where rival families carried clan feuds to extraordinary lengths by barricading themselves inside towers which they then built higher during the night so that they could waken their neighbours with a fusilade of rocks next morning; explore the 9,500-feet-long Vlychada grotto in the Diros Caves, with its breathtaking stalactites and stalagmites (Which is which? 'Tites come down', grinned a toothy guide to my small sons, thereby ensuring that they would remember for ever); or even step back into the half-world of myth and history at Gytheion, once the port of Sparta, where Paris is said to have abducted Helen of Troy.

The road from Sparta leads north to Tripolis, but instead of going round three sides of a square, as this chapter has just done, there is an interesting drive from Pyrgos past Olympia to Tripolis, through the hard and even heartbreaking Arcadian mountains. Historically, this area has had a reputation for harshness, and the scenery backs up the tales. The road, officially described as good, is difficult: a succession of long climbs to the top of a pass, with one feeling that when one reaches the summit the Plain of Tripolis must at last be visible far below. But there always seems to be yet another mountain ahead, and the drive can take several hours.

The way is often precipitous, and matters are not helped by the homicidal behaviour of the drivers of the long-distance buses, their roofs laden with luggage, which are the only means of public transport in this area. It is often necessary to pull on to the verge to let one of these coaches pass, but if there is no verge and you happen to be on a stretch of road with a precipice on one side and a sheer cliff face on the other, the coach driver will still give you no time to take evasive action. An aggressive young Briton who drove across these mountains in a sports car to Tripolis two years ago, and who dared to challenge the coach drivers' right of way, was reduced to a nervous wreck by the Greeks' overt hostility, and completed the journey with a wheel brace in one hand ready to fend off 'attacking' buses.

The mountain villages also present another problem. When I stopped in pretty Langadia to buy bread, cheese and wine for a picnic, the menfolk showed a strong aversion to foreign languages. Seeking directions, I asked several of the villagers if they spoke English. None replied, except for one powerfully-built man with a magnificent white moustache who gazed at me coldly before replying, in perfect English: 'No, I do not speak English. I am Greek.' Then he turned on his heel and walked away. It was a character trait which many British people may recognise. But help, both efficient and inefficient, was at hand. First, in the bakery, a volunteer stepped forward and offered his assistance. 'Yes, I speak English', he said. 'Manchester United. Bobby

Charlton. Bloody good.' An admiring crowd gathered to listen to their neighbour talking to the visitors from overseas, little realising that his vocabulary was of somewhat limited use when it came to ordering bread. Fortunately many Greek families are emigrating, if only temporarily, to Australia, and one of the crowd recognised my predicament. A small boy of about ten pushed through the crowd, and exclaimed in the strident accents of back-street Sydney: 'Well, g'day! You're a pom, aren't you? Can I help you buy your bread?'

Beyond Tripolis lies Nafplion, which is probably the best centre for excursions in the entire Peloponnese. It is an attractive town, overlooking a lovely bay with good hotels and *tavernas.* King Otho set up court on the hill of Palamidi, 857 steps above the town, where the Frankish-Venetian fortress dominates the surrounding area. The picturesque Venetian fort built on the islet of Bourdzi, in the bay, has been converted into a small hotel which was once a home for retired hangmen but is now one of the country's most unusual places in which to stay. Nafplion also boasts what must be the most-underdeveloped tourist attraction in Greece: in the garden of the twelfth-century nunnery of Aghia Moni is the Kanathos fountain in which Hera, the queen of heaven, is said to have bathed once a year to regain her virginity. If it still works, it could turn Nafplion into the spa town to end all spa towns.

Epidaurus, now known principally for its theatre and easily reached from Nafplion 18 miles away, was also famous as a healing sanctuary in former times, and—as at Delphi—strict measures were taken to keep its sanctity and to ensure that birth and death did not occur there. The theatre, beautifully set among the pines, and seating 16,000 people, is still used for performances of Greek tragedy and comedy during the Festival of Drama every summer. Its acoustics are legendary: a remark made in a low voice on the stage can be heard quite clearly at the back of the fifty-fifth tier without the aid of microphones.

Twelve miles away, the ruins of old Epidaurus are now beneath the waves, but can still be visited by skin divers. Other excursions from Nafplion are to Tiryns, probably the most ancient site in mainland Greece, and to Mycenae. Homer spoke of 'walled' Tiryns, and the Cyclopean pre-Hellenic walls, which contain secret passages, can still be seen as well as a tower, vaulted chambers, and several gates. Tiryns is the town where Heracles is supposed to have been born.

A few miles to the north is the site of another famous city-state, Mycenae, an ostensibly severe site which includes the extraordinary beehive tombs. The ruins of the palace fortress which gave its name to the Mycenaean civilisation extend over a large area on the side of a hill. The Acropolis is entered by the famous Lion Gate, where two standing lionesses are depicted on a triangular slab over the lintel; inside one can see the remains of houses, granaries and reservoirs, as well as the graves where many of the golden treasures were found which are now on show in the Mycenaean room in the archaeological museum of Athens. Perhaps the principal attraction of Mycenae is that it is a place which can stir the imagination; the ruins are particularly emotive seen by moonlight (stay in the Xenia hotel on the site, or in the village). Significantly, the reaction of many people who go to Mycenae is to rush straight back to the archaeological museum in Athens to take another look at the Mycenaean room.

Nafplion is also a good 'sun, sea and sand' resort, with nearby Tolon and Drepanon boasting beautiful sandy beaches. A friend sent me hot-foot to Tolon by describing the semi-circular bay on which the village stands as one of the most beautiful in Greece; but unfortunately the property developers got there before I did. Today Tolon is a miniature replica of a typical resort on Spain's Costa Brava: the ugly concrete hotel blocks shading the beach, and the advertising signs replacing the Greek atmosphere with an air of mid-Atlantic jollity. Kosta, Porto Heli, and their mushrooming neighbours are better seaside resorts. From Nafplion a good road back to Corinth completes the circuit of the peninsula.

Of the islands off the coast of the Peloponnese, the best known is probably Hydra, a long bare, rocky and waterless island with a surprisingly attractive port and a reputation for housing writers and painters. Although its tall houses make the town look picturesque, it is a tiring place to move about in because of the innumerable flights of steep steps, and the beaches are poor.

Its rival, Spetsai, is becoming more popular. It is a small, green island which, like its neighbours, can be approached either from Athens (up to five hours on the ferry, or two hours on a very uncomfortable hovercraft), or by *caique* from the Peloponnese mainland. Once one of the most exclusive spots in Greece, Spetsai now has an air of faded elegance which is highlighted by its Napoleonic-style houses. The pretty town spreads inland up a slope, and high rise buildings have been banned. The ferries arrive at the new harbour, but there are villas to let on the east coast facing the mainland, around the old harbour where they build and repair fishing boats. Inland, the roads can be rough, and as there are only four cars on the island there is little incentive to improve them. Transport is by horse and buggy, or in the one dilapidated bus which goes across the island to a beach which is well equipped with *tavernas* and other necessities.

But although it is becoming a holiday island, Spetsai is still unspoiled. Perhaps this is because there is nothing to see or do inland, many of the beaches are shingle, and the local people—all 5,000 of them—still have their feet firmly on the ground. This latter fact can be inferred by the fact that there are 60 churches on the island, and all of them are in use.

Finally Kithira, off the southern coast of the Peloponnese, celebrated as the birthplace of Aphrodite, is another island with a growing number of visitors, particularly Greeks themselves whose example is always worth following. Greek-Cypriots may raise objections, however, for in Cyprus coach tours still stop at a spot near Paphos to show visitors the spot where Cypriots say the goddess arose from the sea.

6. Thessalonika

Once the second city of Byzantium and now the second city of Greece, Thessalonika is a town with two faces. At first sight it is a sprawling and noisome industrial centre built around a huge and polluted bay. But the Byzantine influence has left its mark, and Thessalonika the holiday resort is full of unheralded art treasures while within a short drive are the unspoiled countryside and empty beaches of the Halkidiki peninsula.

In their endless search for 'new' places, hoteliers and airlines alike have recently shown a keen interest in this area of northern Greece—a rugged country which can suddenly give way to soft, gentle scenery as it does in Halkidiki. Thessalonika's importance both as a business centre and as the heart of this growth area is reflected in recently-introduced direct air links with Britain.

Thessalonika is built at the head of the Thermaic Gulf, around one of the few really good harbours in northern Greece. Perhaps because of these geographical advantages, there have been settlements on the spot since 3,000 B.C. But as Greek cities go, Thessalonika itself is comparatively young. It was probably still only a village when Philip of Macedonia and his son, Alexander the Great, held sway over the whole of Greece, and it was not until 315 B.C. that one of Alexander's heirs, General Kassandros, who had declared himself King of Macedonia, did his best to justify his claim to the throne by marrying Alexander's half-sister, Thessaloniki, and founded and named the city in her honour.

The town grew rapidly during the Roman period and became a provincial capital, and by the time that St Paul visited Thessalonika during his second missionary journey (49–52 A.D.) it was already an important city. St Paul established a Christian Church there, and his two famous letters to the Thessalonians are among Christianity's oldest documents. Thessalonika later became an important staging post on the Via Egnatia (the 'Egnatian Way'), the west-east trunk road which the Romans built across what is now Albania, northern Greece, and Thrace, to link Rome with Byzantium.

As the official residence of several Roman governors, Thessalonika enjoyed both the advantages and disadvantages of autocratic rule. The vain Galerius—on whose orders Dimitrius, now patron saint of Thessalonika, was martyred in 306—built an impressive palace, as well as a triumphal arch in his own honour which can still be seen in the centre of the city. Constantine built the harbour, and Theodosius fortified the town.

Theodosius, who had been converted to Christianity, will be remembered for one of the most savage acts of vengeance in history. In 392, while he was away, there was a riot in the city over the use of Germanic Goths as mercenary troops, and the imprisonment of a local hero, and the leader of the Goths and several of his soldiers were lynched. Theodosius's return was awaited with some trepidation, but instead of punishing the rebels an apparently conciliatory Theodosius invited the entire city to attend a Games to be held in his honour at the Hippodrome. When the Hippodrome was full, Theodosius locked the gates and the Gothic troops were let loose to massacre thousands of local citizens. As a Christian, of course, Theodosius later repented his bloodthirsty deed.

In the seventh century Thessalonika became the second city of the Byzantine Empire as well as being an important commercial and spiritual centre. Despite attacks from the north and east it prospered, and the building and decoration of numerous churches —first with mosaics and later with frescoes—was carried out. It is said that at one time there were 365 churches in Thessalonika, but today only 20 remain.

The city became an important Jewish centre when 20,000 Jews were exiled from Spain in 1492 and made their home there, but most of them were deported during the German Occupation of Greece in the Second World War and died in concentration camps.

Many of the old buildings in Thessalonika were destroyed during fighting between Greeks and Turks when the Greeks recaptured the city in 1912, and a big fire in 1917 also caused extensive damage. Yet much remains, and the impression that one can easily form of modern Thessalonika—that it is a city of ugly, square, concrete tower blocks—is false. The point is that you must go out and look for the Roman, Byzantine, and Venetian relics for, like most Greek cities, Thessalonika displays its architectural and archaeological splendours with the casual air of a wealthy man who sees nothing extraordinary in his riches.

Thessalonika is one of the half dozen places in Europe where the airport runway begins right on the edge of the sea, so that on the approach you fly across the bay rapidly losing height and wondering, however hardened an air traveller you may be, whether the pilot really knows what he is doing. But, just as you feel that you are about to touch the waves, there is a reassuring strip of concrete beneath you. The time spent worrying would be better spent on looking out of the aircraft windows and picking out the landmarks of Thessalonika—with pride of place going to the building which has become the symbol of the modern city, the Lefkos Pyrgos, or White Tower.

Today the White Tower seems grey beside the gleaming concrete of the hotel and office blocks lining the seafront—and perhaps it is this, rather than its violent past, which gives the building a strange, evil presence. Once part of the city's sea walls, this fifteenth-century Venetian building has also been known as the Bloody Tower, and as the masters of Thessalonika have changed over the centuries so the tower has witnessed many

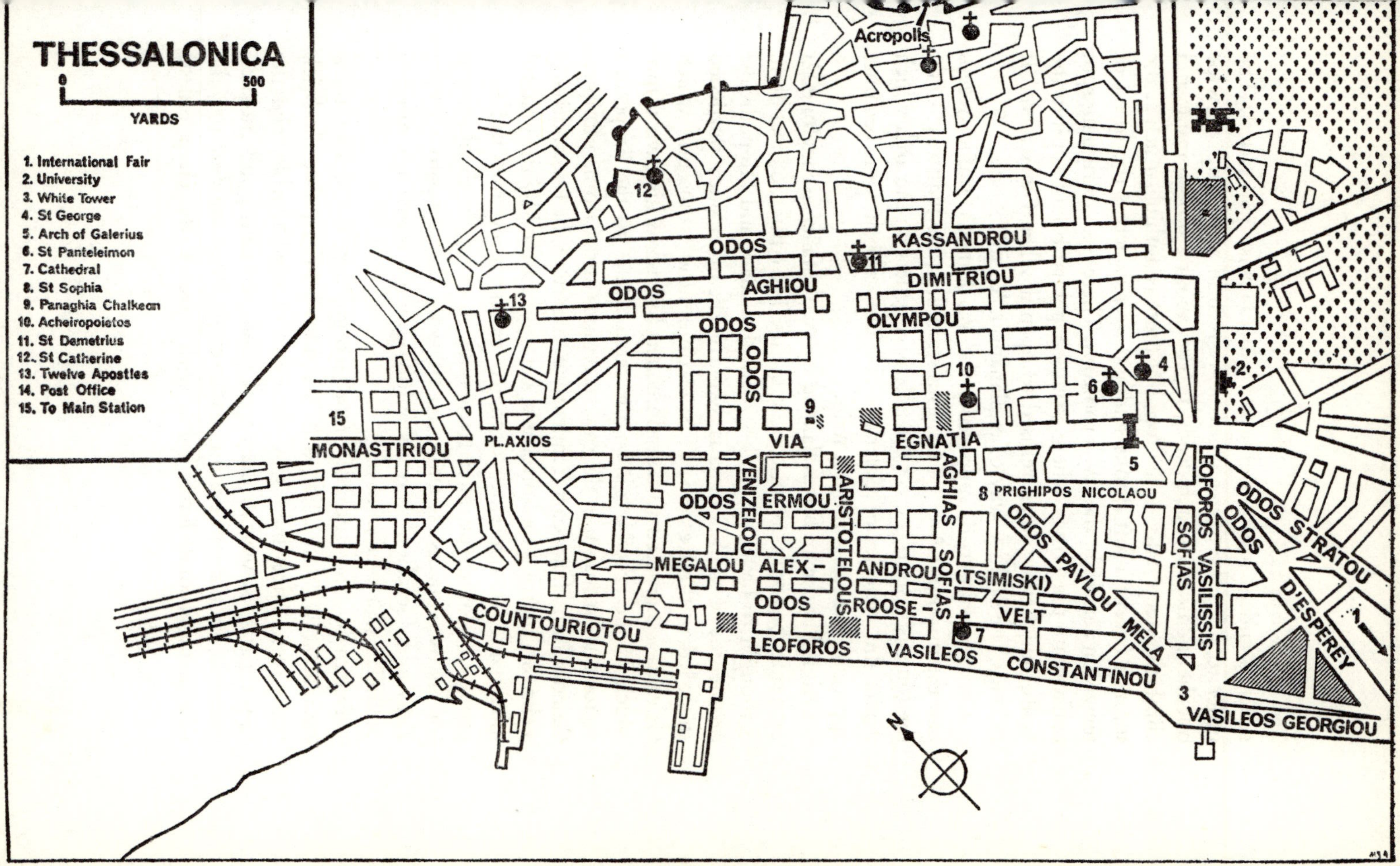
THESSALONICA
0
500
YARDS
1. International Fair
2. University
3. White Tower
4. St George
5. Arch of Galerius
6. St Panteleimon
7. Cathedral
8. St Sophia
9. Panaghia Chalkeon
10. Acheiropoietos
11. St Demetrius
12. St Catherine
13. Twelve Apostles
14. Post Office
15. To Main Station
Acropolis
ODOS KASSANDROU
ODOS AGHIOU DIMITRIOU
ODOS OLYMPOU
ODOS
MONASTIRIOU
PL. AXIOS
VIA EGNATIA
ODOS VENIZELOU
ERMOU
ARISTOTELOUS
AGHIAS SOFIAS
PRIGHIPOS NICOLAOU
ODOS PAVLOU MELA
LEOFOROS VASILISSIS SOFIAS
ODOS STRATOU
ODOS D'ESPEREY
MEGALOU ALEX - ANDROU (TSIMISKI)
ODOS ROOSE - VELT
COUNTOURIOTOU
LEOFOROS VASILEOS CONSTANTINOU
VASILEOS GEORGIOU
N

tortures and at least one massacre (of Turkish janissaries). The order to paint the tower white was given in an attempt to wipe out the memory of such deeds. It costs about 2p to go inside and climb the steep stairs to the top, but there is nothing much at the summit except a soft drinks stall and a view across the forest of television aerials on the city's rooftops. There is an intriguing spot halfway up the Tower where a tiny chapel has been built into the walls, but the custodian refused to open it when I was there. 'It belongs,' he said by way of explanation, 'to the Scouts.'

On the main road, supposedly the Via Egnatia, traffic sweeps past the imposing Arch of Galerius straddling the highway. Only the tourists stop to inspect the extensive reliefs on the arch which depict the victories of Galerius. The Emperor, it soon becomes apparent, was not a modest man.

Originally the arch was flanked by two smaller arches, one on each side, but only one of these remains. The edifice, 68 feet high, is thought to have been linked with the palace and Hippodrome on one side of the Via Egnatia, while on the other side a porticoed street led to the Rotunda of St George, now a museum, which Galerius is supposed to have intended for use as his own tomb. Much of the relief work on the Arch relates to the Emperor's victorious campaign in the eastern regions of the Roman Empire. Galerius himself appears frequently in the frieze: he is seen driving a chariot; fighting on horseback; being welcomed by the grateful inhabitants of a recently occupied town; being merciful to a group of women prisoners; attending a service of thanksgiving for his own successes; and even enjoying the company of both Zeus and Heracles. It is an autobiography which no modern politician will ever surpass.

Externally, the Rotunda of St George, with its 20 feet. thick circular wall, would not win any beauty prizes. But the brick walls were once lined with slabs of coloured marble, and the upper parts, as well as the barrel vaults, contain good mosaics. After the monument became a church in about the year 400, the Christians decorated the dome with mosaics (the city's oldest) which are divided into eight sections, each corresponding to one of the eight recesses. In front of imaginary scenery made up of architectural fantasies, peacocks, and hanging lamps, are grouped saints in twos or threes. The mosaic which was at the centre of the dome has disappeared but, as in other domes, it was probably a figure of Christ within a circle supported by angels. The barrel vaults mosaics depict branches, fruits, flowers, birds, and geometric designs. These mosaics survived the Rotunda's sixteenth-century conversion into a mosque by the occupying Turks, when it was given a faintly jaunty air by the addition of a minaret. Today it is no longer used for worship, but serves as a museum of Christian art.

From the Eptapirgion, the Castle of the Seven Towers, the ruined but still impressive walls of Thessalonika descend to the well-equipped university and the extensive grounds on which the annual International Fair takes place every September. Indeed, the city really comes into its own in the autumn, for besides the fair there is the Festival of Art and Drama in October, a modern revival of an ancient festival held in honour of St Demetrius, during which some of the classic Greek tragedies are performed in the theatre of the Society of Macedonian Studies on the waterfront.

Also worth visiting is the fourteenth-century monastery of Vlatadon, high on the cliff where St Paul preached just outside the Eptapirgion, with its breathtaking view across the town to the faraway peaks of Olympus. In town, the Archaeological Museum contains gold and silver treasure of considerable interest.

Thessalonika's crowning glory, however, is her Byzantine churches, and each is impressive in its own way. To my mind the most splendid of them all is Aghia (St) Sophia, built between 690 and 730 and containing two magnificent mosaics. To see this church at all calls for a certain amount of fortitude and determination. It is closed on Mondays, there is no nameplate outside, and the custodian inside will switch on the floodlighting of the mosaics in the dome and the apse only upon receipt of a suitable mixture of threats, pleading, and cajolery. The effort is worthwhile: the justly famous ninth-century mosaic in the dome represents the Ascension, while the later rendering of the Virgin Mary in the apse (completed with meticulous attention to perspective despite the concave surface) has an unforgettable and haunting beauty.

There are also fine mosaics in the fifth-century Panaghia Ahiropiitos ('Our Lady Made Without Hands')—named after a miraculous ikon which has long since disappeared—and in the apparently modern church of Aghios Dimitrios, a triple-naved basilica which was originally built over the saint's tomb in the fifth century but has had to be rebuilt three times after fires, the last in 1917.

The only surviving medieval guild church, Panaghia Halkeon ('Our Lady of the Coppersmiths') is a graceful brick building erected in 1042 in typical Byzantine Greek cross style. Also worth seeing are Aghii Apostoli (the 'Church of the Holy Apostles') with its five-domed roof and ornamental brickwork; the fifth-century mosaics in the Church of St David, part of the Latomou Monastery; and the frescoes in the Church of Aghios Nikolaos the Orphan, which escaped Turkish conversion into a mosque.

In the soft, candlelit interiors of these historic churches, the events of Thessalonika's tumultuous past do not seem far away. It comes almost as a physical blow to step outside and find oneself back in the twentieth century, in a city where latter-day Thessalonians gather in the pavement cafes for an early evening glass of *ouzo* or, dressed in their Sunday best, take a traditional stroll, or *volta*, along the waterfront between the White Tower and the gardens surrounding the new Macedonia Palace Hotel. I can recommend this hotel, but have not tried the city's only other Luxury-grade hotel, the Mediterranean Palace, which is older and more central. There are a number of far cheaper but modern 'B'-

9 Delphi: the Theatre

grade hotels near the town centre, but some are in rather noisy spots. Generally, there is still a scarcity of rooms in the city.

Restaurants vary enormously. Centrally, you can still eat well and comparatively cheaply at places like the Olympus-Naoussa, choosing from an international menu, but—in a country where the locals like to sit late over dinner—the night life of the town can only be described as prim. The neon lights over one establishment proclaim it to be a 'Sexy Bar'—but you could take a Sunday School outing there with a clear conscience. Just as sexy, and far cheaper, are the out-of-town *tavernas*, where a glass of *ouzo* costs one sixth of what you will be charged in an hotel bar, and where you can eat and drink well all evening for the price of a round of drinks in Britain.

In the summer, many of the townspeople like to go up into the cooler, mountain villages above the city to eat, and the aptly-named Panorama has already become a fashionable suburb with good *tavernas*. Farther west, Oreokastron is popular. But night life generally centres on the seafront, which smells vaguely of sewage, and the open-air cinemas and restaurants.

Also on the seafront are such tourist 'essentials' as the tourist office and the airline offices. The main shopping area lies behind the seafront and, as befits a city of its importance, Thessalonika has a good range of shops. Best buys are embroidery, rugs, and woollen shoulder bags.

Despite the size of the bay on which this city of 450,000 people is built, the all-too-obvious pollution means that visitors must look elsewhere for beaches. Boats from Thessalonika run a shuttle service to the popular nearby beaches at Epivaton, Aretsou, Aghia Trias, and Perea, all privately operated by the Greek tourist organisation, E.O.T. Although fairly crowded, these E.O.T. beaches are something of a bargain: in return for a very

10 Thessalonika: the Arch of Galerius

11 Thessalonika: the Rotunda of St George

small entrance fee you get sands which are cleaned daily, safe bathing, changing rooms, showers, deckchairs, sun umbrellas, a children's playground, and a cafeteria.

There are good camping sites at Aretsou and Aghia Trias, the latter a handy 27 km out of town. Other beaches worth looking at are at Nea Mihaniona and Epanomi, while the Thermaikos Beach is crowded, picturesque, and popular.

How much better, though, to find your own beach and to sunbathe and swim in utter solitude. In northern Greece, with a hired car, you can do just that; within an hour you can be on the sandy shore of some remote village far to the south of Thessalonika. In two hours you can be in the heart of the Halkidiki peninsula, and there—even though the developers have beaten you to it—there is still room to be alone.

7. The Halkidiki Peninsula

Drive south from Thessalonika, past the string of beaches used by the people of Greece's second city, and you find yourself heading into rolling countryside more reminiscent of Rhodes, or one of the other medium-sized islands, than anywhere on the mainland. Within an hour you are deep in the countryside of the Halkidiki Peninsula, where tiny, half-forgotten villages hug the coastline and where, near places like Nea Kalikatria, you can always find half a mile or more of sandy beach entirely to yourself.

Halkidiki, poking tentatively into the Aegean like a three-fingered hand, is one of the last 'undiscovered' holiday areas in Greece—an under-used and under-developed peninsula which is almost separated from the rest of the country by two big lakes, Koronia and Volvi, and which is ideal for personal voyages of exploration. As if beaches, pine woods, and green hills were not enough, Halkidiki also contains the autonomous religious republic of Mount Athos—the most easterly of the three 'fingers'—where the 20 monasteries are a remote treasure-house of Byzantine art. Mount Athos is a fitting climax to any tour of the peninsula, but to visit the 'Holy Mountain' you will need a permit which can be obtained from the Greek Foreign Ministry, in Athens, or the Regional Administration Department of Northern Greece in Thessalonika; and women are banned from this all-male preserve.

Although Mount Athos has had a smattering of visitors for

some time, many of them cruise passengers on excursions and seeing only one or two of the monasteries, the rest of the Halkidiki peninsula is relatively unknown. It has been opened up very recently by the growth of international flights into Thessalonika, the availability of holiday car-hire 'packages' like British Airways' 'Fly-Drive' and 'Freewheeler' schemes, and the development of resort complexes like Porto Carras on the central 'finger', Sithonia.

Even if you have never driven abroad before, you will find no problems on the empty roads of Halkidiki. Indeed, the area seems ready-made for go-as-you-please holidays.

If you do not deliberately follow the coastal road, heading for the beaches, all paths seem to lead automatically to the centrally-situated provincial capital, Poligiros, built like an amphitheatre at the foot of the green Mount Holomon. Poligiros is a brisk commercial centre, noted for its weaving and its typically Macedonian architecture, and with a good archaeological museum. From the mountain there are sweeping views of the whole peninsula.

To the south of Poligiros, the roads head towards the three 'fingers': Kassandra, Sithonia, and Mount Athos.

There is evidence that the Halkidiki peninsula has been inhabited since as long ago as 80,000 B.C., and a paleolithic skull was discovered not long ago in the 'Red Cave' at Petraolona, near Nea Kalikratia. Paleolithic man knew what he was doing when he settled near Kassandra, for it is a lovely promontory ringed with white sands along thickly-wooded shores. Modern Potidea, on the narrow isthmus, is built on the site of a Corinthian colony of the same name, and along the coast are a string of pretty fishing villages like Afitos, Kalithea, Kriopigi, and Kapsohora, where the local *tavernas* serve delicious fresh seafood.

There are yachting stations and camping sites along the coast, although you can of course camp anywhere provided that you have the landowner's permission and also that you notify the local police—two regulations which are unlikely to be very rigorously enforced in this free-and-easy part of the country unless you are doing any damage to property. Just outside Paliourion, on the southernmost tip of Kassandra, there is a Xenia tourist complex in a lovely setting. From here, the road doubles back on itself to head north again through another string of fishing villages. There is an interesting walk between Nea Skioni and Mendi, down to a coastline guarded by tall towers which used to be used to watch for pirates. In the inland village of Kassandra, after which this stretch of the peninsula is named, there is a well-preserved windmill and a tall bell-tower topped by a nest built by visiting storks.

Sithonia, the central one of the three promontories, is even quieter and, if possible, even lovelier than Kassandra. Its wooded inlets, burrowing into the pinewoods, give the impression of an embroidered coastline spiked by trees. There is a new road down the western side of the promontory, but otherwise access to the more remote villages is by dirt-track—a fact which Greeks will blithely explain away by saying: 'The road network is not yet complete.'

In fact, until recently, Sithonia was dying. The population, already sparse, was shrinking and many of the fishing villages were decaying. Tourists could find nothing in the way of amenities, although—as almost everywhere in Greece—it was and is still possible to rent a spotlessly-clean room in a private house very cheaply indeed. Now, however, an immense agricultural and tourist development is taking shape near the village of Neos Marmaras, halfway down the west coast of the promontory.

It is called Porto Carras, and covers a 10,000-acre site where life is, almost literally, being breathed back into the community. Whatever one may think of developments of this kind in a totally unspoilt area, there are many points in favour of Porto Carras. A total of 70,000 olive trees have been planted on the site, and light industry—in the form of olive presses, and the beginnings of a wine-producing set-up—has been introduced. With all this has come a holiday village for 3,000 visitors, a yacht marina, a golf course, and an impressive array of restaurants. 'It started as a very big farm, and tourism came as a natural consequence,' says Telemaque Maratos, a director of the company responsible for the project. 'This area was inaccessible and, for all practical purposes, forgotten. We have drained a swamp, and built 100 km of road. But you needn't worry—we are not turning it into another Costa Brava, and everything is being done artistically.'

The road to the third promontory, Mount Athos, runs through the village of Arnea, well-known for its wines and for the textiles woven by the women: carpets, rugs, blankets, and long-pile 'flocates' or rugs which make fine souvenirs. Stagira, farther along the road, was the birthplace of Aristotle, and as the vista of Mount Athos—'the Garden of the Holy Virgin'—opens up ahead the promontory narrows to a narrow isthmus at Nea Roda, with its tiny and picturesque harbour. It was here that Xerxes cut a canal rather than risk his fleet in the winds and currents off the southern cape of Mount Athos.

At Ouranoupolis the road ends, and you can catch a boat from there to Dafni, the port serving Karies which is the capital of the monks' republic. There is a Xenia Hotel at Ouranoupolis, in which visitors can stay before exploring Mount Athos; an alternative way of reaching the monasteries is direct by boat from Thessalonika.

Entry rules are strict. The 'no women' rule, although it may seem harsh in these days of female emancipation, is seen by the monks as a considerable relaxation of earlier edicts, which demanded that all male visitors should be bearded, and that 'no females' were allowed on the mountain—and that included animals! Today you do not need to wait at Ouranoupolis while your whiskers grow, for any male over 21 and armed with the necessary papers will be admitted, and males under 21 can also go on to the mountain as long as they are accompanied by elders. Filming and tape-recording in the monasteries is forbidden, although ordinary still photographs are permitted.

In Karies, your papers are exchanged for a *diamonitirion*, an impressive document which has to be handed to the *archontaris*

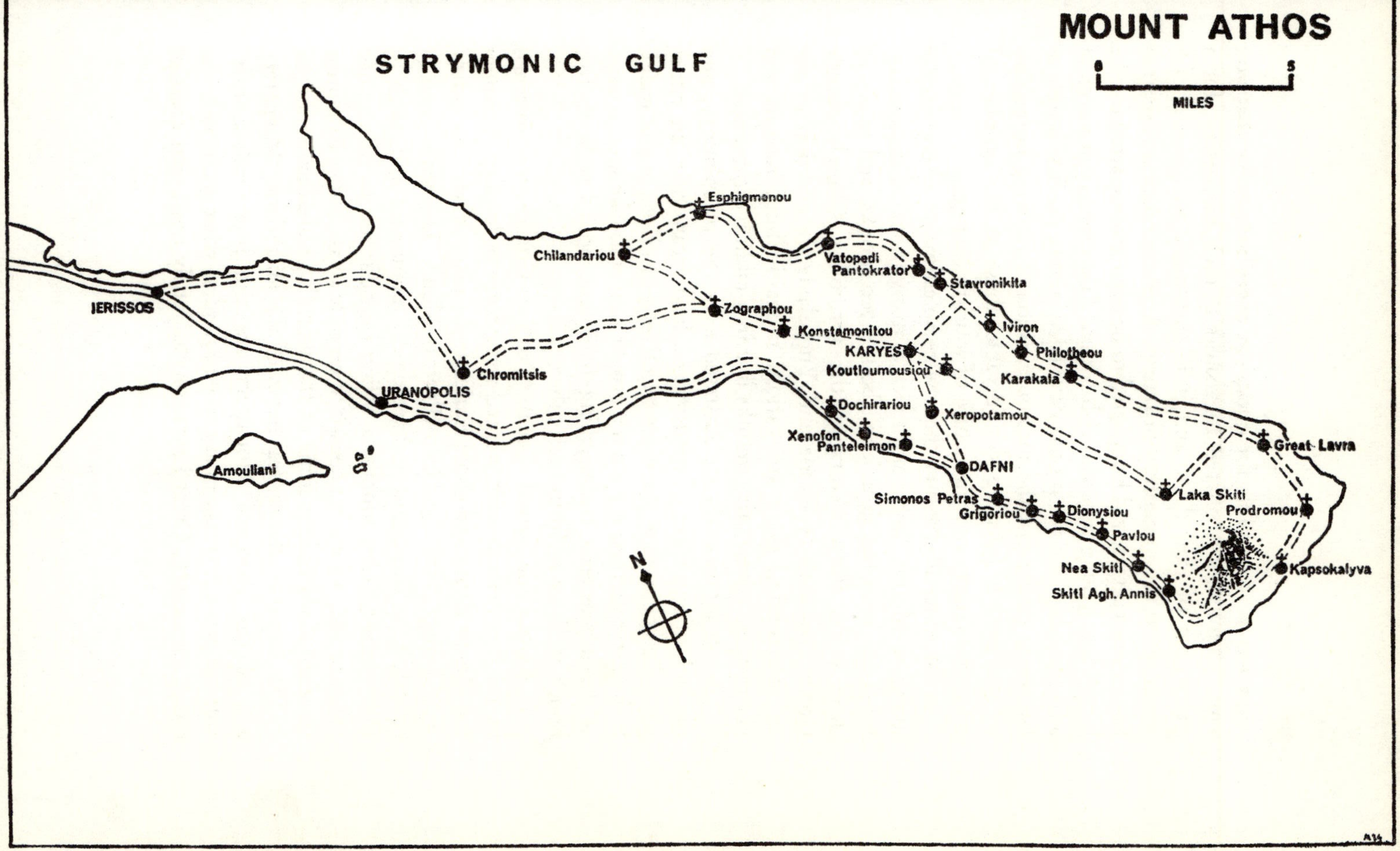
MOUNT ATHOS
0
5
MILES
STRYMONIC GULF
Esphigmenou
Chilandariou
Vatopedi
Pantokrator
Stavronikita
IERISSOS
Zographou
Konstamonitou
Iviron
KARYES
Philotheou
Koutloumousiou
Karakala
Chromitsis
URANOPOLIS
Dochirariou
Xeropotamou
Xenofon
Panteleimon
DAFNI
Great Lavra
Amouliani
Laka Skiti
Simonos Petras
Grigoriou
Dionysiou
Prodromou
Pavlou
Nea Skiti
Kapsokalyva
Skiti Agh. Annis
N

—the monk responsible for guests—at every monastery that you visit. Hospitality is offered to visitors at each monastery, for a maximum of two days, and it is customary to make a cash donation to the monastery in return. Accommodation is spartan for serious visitors, and is reported to be even more spartan for the hippy-type youngsters who visit Mount Athos merely in search of a free holiday—for the monks have been among the first people in Greece to realise that the ancient tradition of showing hospitality to strangers is open to considerable abuse as the number of tourists increases and the nature of tourism changes.

In the sixteenth century there were an estimated 40,000 monks living on Mount Athos, and twice as many monasteries as today. Now the total has shrunk to about 1,700 monks, and many of these come from sectors of the Orthodox Church outside Greece, particularly Russia and Yugoslavia. In addition to the 20 monasteries, there are various monastic huts, retreats and hermitages, where other monks live in a biblical atmosphere.

The 20 monasteries are scattered over the promontory, and the lack of any form of transport on land means that one either visits the 15 closest to the shore selectively, by *caique*, or else walks. If the latter method is chosen a proper tour will take several days, as the monasteries are anything from one hour's walk to five hour's walk away from each other.

In Karies, one should visit the Protatos Church, so christened by the first hermits who wanted some form of local government for Mount Athos and chose Karies as the place where the 'elders' would meet with the Head (Protos) Monk. The tenth-century church is an important archaeological monument and, with its fourteenth-century murals, a fitting introduction to this unique religious state which has chosen to become a vast, living Byzantine museum shyly hiding some of the world's greatest art treasures.

The mural of the central naves of the Hilandarios Monastery and of the Vatopedi Monastery are also fourteenth-century. But the greatest treasures are to be found in what is officially the oldest monastery, Great Lavra, on the lonely north-east coast of the promontory beneath the peak of Mount Athos itself. Great Lavra, built in 963, has an extremely rich library, is stuffed with sacred relics, and also contains some beautiful frescoes by Theophanes the Cretan who, with his son, became a monk there in the sixteenth century and founded the Cretan school of painting. Theophanes' disciplined work is in contrast to the naturalism of fourteenth-century work, and there are further examples of both his murals and his icons in Stavronikita Monastery. The central church at Great Lavra also has a magnificent twelfth-century fresco in the dome which, like most of the treasures of Mount Athos, has escaped both the ravages of time and despoliation during the long Turkish occupation.

Vatopedi claims to be the oldest-established monastery on Mount Athos, for it is said to have been founded in 383. The present buildings, close to the shore on the north-east coast, date from the eleventh and sixteenth centuries. The monastery contains the miraculous thirteenth-century icon of Panaghia the Esphagmeni ('massacred') which is said to have poured with blood when struck with a knife by an angry church deacon. Another icon, Panaghia the Antiphonitra, is claimed to have ordered an empress to leave its church, and is one of a number of icons credited with the power of speech.

Other 'miraculous' icons are among the many early examples in the other monasteries. The monasteries themselves are often dramatically situated: Aghiou Dionysiou is on a steep rock by the sea on the south-western side of the promontory, and Pantokrator —which has a richly-coloured and very emotive fourteenth-century fresco of the Macedonian school—is built in a picturesque spot where it manages to convey the impression of rising out of the sea. Most dramatic of all is the Simonos Petras monastery, built on a rock 1,100 feet high and with a cliff-face appearing to fall away sheer below its windows. It is a half-hour climb from the sea, and its frescoes have been almost totally destroyed by three disastrous fires, but it does contain a relic alleged to be the left hand of Mary Magdalene. It is usually visited, however, principally for its setting, for it is a building which, perhaps above all others, seems to form a bridge between the earth and the sky—a role which might also be attributed to Mount Athos.

Depending upon their time and interests, visitors will find their own favourities among the monasteries of Mount Athos. Many, because of lack of time, will only be able to view them from the sea—and will be missing something unique. Women are limited to this sea view, and as if fearing some unmentionable retaliation for this sex bar, Brother Andreas Theophilopoulos, secretary of the holy community, has issued this warning in his admirable *Guide to Mount Athos*:

> It is recommended that women sailing around Athos be dressed decently out of reverence for the sacredness of the area. Also, none of them should attempt to approach the sacred rocks, especially those of Karoulia, where the residents, having purified themselves through the exercising of virtue, have neither seen any women, nor have they heard female talk or laughter for decades, for instead of blessings such women will receive the curses of the Athos Fathers.

8. Northern and Central Greece

Much of mainland Greece, and especially the northern and central areas, is virtually unknown to tourists—and even allowing for the steady increase of holiday motoring in Greece, this state of affairs seems likely to continue for some time to come. Much of the central and north-west of the country is mountainous, with the huge Mount Olympus range effectively splitting the country in two; roads can be bad; and the winter weather is often very harsh. The plains of Thessaly and Thrace are places which one goes through rather than to. And yet, as always in Greece, these areas have an attractive individuality which it is a pity to miss, quite apart from their scenic and archaeological wonders.

One of the archaeological wonders is the old Roman road, the Via Egnatia, or Egnatian Way, which cuts across the Balkan peninsula to link Rome with Constantinople. Today the road lies partly in Albania and partly, of course, in Turkey, and northern Greece lacks a true-east highway. One can start out from the western port of Igoumenitsa and pick up the route of the old road farther to the north, but it is more usually followed from Thessalonika into Thrace, or for excursions from Thessalonika into such lovely Macedonian towns as Edessa, Naoussa, or Kastoria.

Kastoria, in the centre of northern Greece, is the town near which motorists driving from Igoumenitsa will pick up the route of the old Roman road. It is known as 'the city of the lake' because it is built on a promontory jutting out into a lake also called Kastoria, and it is a small but very scenic town. The road then goes north to Florina, a busy commercial centre close to the Yugoslav border at Niki. Because northern Greece remained under Turkish domination for much longer than the rest of the country, and because the Balkans are a racial melting pot anyway, this area seems to have a confused culture all of its own and made up of Turkish and Slavonic influences as well as Greek.

Florina, said to have been founded by Philip of Macedonia, is surrounded by pine-clad mountains and is a growing handicrafts centre. Fruit also flourishes in this area, and there is a big honey-producing industry in Macedonia. From Florina, the modern road continues east, around the northern shores of Lake Vegoritis, to the beautiful resort town of Edessa—'the town of the waterfalls'.

High on a green plateau overlooking fertile plains, Edessa's setting is made even more attractive because the River Vodas runs through the town as a series of streams and waterfalls, a combination which makes it both picturesque and pleasantly cool in summer. The town is popular with Greeks, and its atmosphere is already in danger of being spoiled as caverns are turned into discotheques and as the spring festival, the 'Anthestiria', when the townspeople don local costume and dance to folk tunes, develops into a tourist attraction. But Edessa, a dream-like oasis rich in every kind of fruit and with a strange, misty atmosphere which reminds one of childhood pictures of the Garden of Eden, has only just made its mark on the holidaymakers' map—and excesses worse than a disco or two are undoubtedly to come.

From Edessa it is a 55-mile drive down to Thessalonika, but it is worth making a detour to the south to visit Naoussa, another charming little town surrounded by cascading streams and famous for its Brousko red wine. The wine may help to explain the town's particularly energetic spring carnival.

Just outside Thessalonika is Pella, the ancient Macedonian capital and birthplace of Alexander the Great. Excavations there are comparatively recent, but several public buildings have been uncovered, and the courtyards were found to contain interesting pebble mosaics including one which tells the story of Helen of Troy. Most of the mosaics are now in the museum, as are two other much-prized finds from the site: a vase depicting the battle of the Amazons, and a bronze statuette of Poseidon. Between Pella and Thessalonika a main road leads north to Evzoni on the Yugoslav border—a favourite entry point for motorists making the long road journey to Greece, but also a spot where many people must form unhappy first impressions of the country because of the aggressive attitude taken by the customs and immigration officials on the Greek side of the border.

Thrace, the narrow coastal stretch of countryside which separates Bulgaria from the sea, and where Greece has a common border with European Turkey, has some fine scenery—particularly between the port of Kavala and Xanthi—as well as such historic sites as Philippi. The area to the east of Thessalonika also has its oddities: in the little town of Langadas a religious sect put themselves into a deep trance every year on May 21 and then dance barefoot on a bed of red-hot coals without any apparent ill effects.

But for the most part Thrace exhibits all the characteristics of a backward agricultural area whose inhabitants have rarely been as far as Thessalonika, let alone Athens. The people are not always friendly, and it is hard to get to know them. Marriage is the chief concern of the women, and any female tourist who is single and over the age of 18 is likely to be a source of bewilderment and even pity—'Don't you *want* to get married?' one 21-year-old was asked. Every village has its evening *volta*—the boys parading arm-in-arm with each other, and the girls doing the same, and no 'unattached' couple ever going out alone together.

After Athens, Kavala is probably the most beautiful town in Grcccc. It is built on thc foothills of Mount Symvolon, looking across towards the island of Thasos, and has a colourful port which serves a big fish market and is also the centre of the region's tobacco trade. The sixteenth-century Kamares aqueduct curves across the town below the crumbling remains of a Byzantine fortress, and can hardly be missed. Kavala has a good beach and camping site, and boats run from there and from the port of Keramoti to Thasos, the wooded island which is the most northerly in the Aegean. Circular trips tour Thasos, which has some very good beaches and is rapidly being developed into a tourist resort with first-class hotel and bungalow installations.

From Kavala, the 'Via Egnatia' runs on for 111 miles to Alexandroupolis, the most easterly town in Greece, which is a comparatively modern port devoid of any particularly interesting characteristics but with a good choice of hotels and restaurants. En route, and particularly at Xanthi, the towns and villages take on a markedly oriental appearance, with a flowering of minarets and women dressed in the full Turkish-style trousers. Rather more interesting is the road to the north of Kavala, which leads through ancient Philippi to the Plain of Drama—'the golden plain' as the Turks called it, because of the landscape's colouring in the light of early evening. It might better have been called 'the plain of blood', for Greeks, Romans, Turks and Bulgars have battled for centuries at this Balkan crossroads.

Philippi, known to all students of Shakespeare as the scene of the battle in which Mark Antony and Octavius defeated Brutus and Cassius in 42 B.C., was originally established by Philip of Macedonia, who wanted to protect some gold mines in the area and gave the colony his own name. It is also the spot from which St Paul set out on his mission to preach Christianity in Greece. Today there are the remains of a fifth-century basilica and many Roman remains to be seen, as well as an acropolis with extensive views.

A tree-lined avenue leads on to Drama, a brisk little tobacco-growing town with the remains of a Roman wall and a small Byzantine church. Serve, to the west, has an acropolis on top of which are the ruins of a thirteenth-century castle with a Byzantine church in the walls and a crypt with a secret entrance.

But strange buildings like this are nothing to the buildings which can be found in the very centre of mainland Greece, and which make even Mount Athos look ordinary: the pinnacled monasteries of the Meteora.

The area–western Thessaly–is reached by road from Athens via Lamia and Trikala, the latter being at the heart of the fertile plain of Thessaly which was an inland sea in prehistoric times. There are also bus and train links with Athens.

Trikala shares with Macedonia a violent past, for the fierce fighting men of the surrounding mountains staged many uprisings when Trikala was a Turkish capital during the occupation, and Trikala itself was frequently destroyed. As a result there is little in the way of archaeological remains in the town itself, although there is a Byzantine fortress on top of the wooded Kastro hill, and some good views of the plain. Trikala, once an important medical centre like Epidaurus and Kos, does have two good churches and the extraordinary Koursoum Mosque built in 1550. The museum, and the colourful old quarter of the town with its old mansion houses, are worth exploring, and there are good excursions to the sixteenth-century Monastery of Doussikos (which has a cell for each day of the year) and the Porta Panaghia monastery.

A tree-lined road leads to Kalambaka, the town used as a base by most visitors to the Meteora and blessed with a railway station and modern hotels, restaurants and shops. There is a good view from the Xenia Hotel across to the Meteora itself, an extraordinary forest of upright rocks jutting out of the ground and sometimes topped by a monastery despite the angle at which the rock may be tilted.

The great grey rocks, each separate from its neighbour and often torn by cracks and caves, became a religious refuge in the fourteenth century, when hermits found peace in this dramatic landscape. The earliest hermitage is Panaghia Doupiani, and one of the hermits, Neilos, built four other churches on the surrounding rocks between 1358 and 1368. Gradually other buildings sprang up and were turned into monasteries, for the area was considered to be safe from robbers and–with the introduction of a regulation in the 1360s that no women were allowed there—safe from temptation too. By the sixteenth century there were 24 monasteries in all, but today only four of them are inhabited. They are remarkable for their domed roofs, their wooden galleries, and for the way in which their upper storeys project precariously out into space. Access to the monasteries used to be by ladder, or by means of a net lowered from these upper storeys, but narrow paths have now been hewn out of the rock to provide a more formal entrance.

The largest monastery, Great Meteoro—after which the area was named—was built between 1356 and 1372 and was once very rich. It is still occupied, as are Varlaam (containing sixteenth-century frescoes and a fine Byzantine icon of the Virgin), Aghia Triada (140 steps up on one of the most beautiful rocks), and Aghios Stefanos (the most southerly of the monasteries, with fifteenth-century frescoes and an interesting museum). Aghios Stefanos is cut off from the world by a deep ravine, and was the last monastery to continue using a basket and a rope as a means of access. Modern visitors will be glad to know that a bridge has now been erected across the ravine. Also worth noting is the rock known as the Pillar of Doupiani, on top of which is a twelfth-century chapel and two somewhat inaccessible monasteries.

In all, this is an area rich in religious history—a history which contrasts with its violent past and with the physical appearance of the hard, sheepskin-coated men from the mountains who you will find seated outside the *tavernas* of the surrounding villages. The monks had an explanation. In this lovely landscape, they said, they found the meaning of God.

Although not every visitor with his own car or a hired vehicle will get as far as Meteora, the west coast of the Greek mainland between the port of Igoumenitsa, opposite Corfu, and the big ferry terminal at Patras is being increasingly explored by holidaymakers.

12 Corfu: Mouse Island in background

Igoumenitsa itself is at the head of a long, narrow gulf, and is well equipped with hotels and restaurants. A re-routed 'Via Egnatia' leads to Ioanina, 64 miles inland. A clean, modern, lakeside town with a distinctly Italian appearance, Ioanina suddenly becomes Eastern European when you venture into the old walled town or the main shopping area, where worthwhile souvenirs include metalwork (especially silver) and embroidered goods. The town was once the stronghold of the formidable Turkish leader, Ali Pasha, and there is an Asian museum. The lake, officially known as Pamvotis Lake but more often called after the town, is a popular centre for water sports and sailing during the summer. The nearby Perama Cave, with its big stalactitites and stalagmites, is an interesting excursion.

A few miles north-west of Ioanina is the seldom-visited mountain village of Zitsa, which Byron described as 'the prettiest place in Greece'. It is certainly a quaint spot, with multi-storeyed houses lining the narrow streets and lots of flower-filled balconies. The local vineyards produce a light, sparkling wine which is served—corked and capped like a bottle of beer—in the village's one restaurant which has the very un-Greek name of The Black Cat.

Travelling south from Igoumenitsa, motorists would be foolish not to make the slight detour off the main road—along which fish eagles sit as though on sentry duty—to visit the lovely little seaside resort of Parga, which has two fine beaches shaded by ancient olive trees, a thirteenth-century Norman castle, and a harbour with an island in it. Parga is a popular destination for Greek day-trippers from both Igoumenitsa and Patras, but it does not get crowded during the week.

The main road goes either to Preveza, at the mouth of a large inlet which must be crossed by ferry, or else turns inland to bustling Arta, former capital of a Byzantine principality and

13 *Patmos: view from the Monastery of St John*

dominated by a medieval fortress as well as several carefully restored examples of Byzantine architecture. But historians will not lose by choosing the Preveza route, for the town has links with Roman Actium, and its ruins include the fine walls, two theatres, and the traces of a temple. There is a rent-a-tent campsite near the town, and the harbourside is ringed with tavernas which again specialise in a light, sparkling wine produced locally. An hourly ferry crosses to Aktion, on the southern shore of the inlet, and the fare is only a few pence.

From Aktion the road along the southern shore of the inlet—the Ambracian Gulf—is a lonely, bumpy ride to Vonitsa and Amphilohia, two old lakeland towns frequented mainly by huntsmen in search of water fowl. Armed with a camera, you can hunt among the reeds for wild geese, duck, and coots. Amphilohia is another town which will bring back memories of the Italian lakes, but it is a very unsophisticated spot where visitors may well have problems in changing travellers' cheques if only because many of the restaurateurs and shopkeepers have never seen one before. Bathing in the gulf here at night has an odd effect: you may come out shimmering and glowing because of the phosphorescence in the water.

There are more lakes bordering the road down to the industrial town of Agrinion—an area where the storks have moved in en masse, nesting on church towers, electricity pylons, and every other tall structure in sight. You reach the sea again at the fishing port of Etolikon. To the north, a side road leads up to Astakos, a good spear-fishing centre with pebbly beaches and lots of rocky coves. The main road goes south for the few miles to Missolonghi—the town whose heroic resistance during the Greek War of Independence captured the imagination of the Great Powers and finally led to the expulsion of the Turks. It is also the town where Byron died of a fever while fighting as a volunteer with the defence forces.

Today, heroic Missolonghi is just another quiet fishing village—although the past is remembered in the Park of the Heroes, and in the small museum which can be found in the Town Hall. For refreshment, the *tavernas* in the town specialise in spit-roasted fresh fish and eels, and in *avgotaracho*, the Greek equivalent of caviare.

The final destination of this journey down the western side of the Greek mainland is Nafpaktos, an attractive Venetian port with two small castles guarding the entrance to its little harbour. A square lined with plane trees opens on to the harbour, with its open-air cafés and restaurants, and there is a good choice of hotel accommodation. Regular car ferries link Nafpaktos and Antirion with Rion on the Peloponnese peninsula, a half-hour's journey across the Gulf of Corinth which is very narrow at this point. Meanwhile the main road swings inland and heads up towards the mountains and Delphi.

9. Corfu and the Ionian Islands

'There are,' said Spyros Lychnos reflectively, 'many beautiful girls in Corfu.' Apparently cheered by this thought, he picked up his glass from the metal-topped table in front of us and took a long sip of cold beer. His business partner, whose name is also Spyros (more than half of the men in Corfu are called Spyros, for reasons which will soon become apparent), nodded in agreement, his eyelids drooping heavily and sensuously over his eyes in what might have been a wink or might merely have signified the onset of sleep. All around us on the Esplanade in Corfu Town —walking, talking, puttering past on mopeds, hailing friends and acquaintances, salty from the sea and bronzed by the summer sun —holidaymakers and locals alike provided visual evidence in support of the truth of Mr Lychnos's statement: there *are* many beautiful girls in Corfu.

The Spyros duo run a travel agency in the main town of Corfu —or 'Kerkira', as the Greeks prefer to call it—and represent a number of British holiday firms on the island. They had accordingly been among my first contacts in Corfu and now, after a long, hot day at work, they were introducing me to one of the country's most traditional pastimes: the evening stroll, or *volta*.

The role of the *volta* changes depending upon what part of Greece you are in and what day of the week it is. In the big cities, especially on summer Sunday evenings, it is a fashion parade for which everyone puts on their finest clothes; in rural areas it can still be a sort of open-air marriage market, with the over-protected girls having perhaps their only chance of the day to smile shyly at some eligible young man.

But in cosmopolitan Corfu Town the *volta*, along the colonnaded west side of the central square and up beside the park, is simply a recognition that the heat of the day is over and that it is time for a breath of fresh air and perhaps a cool drink. As dusk falls, and the swifts wheel and scream over the narrow streets and the peeling buildings, there could be nothing more pleasant than sipping a glass of beer outside one of the many tiny bars and—literally—watching the world go by. The numbers of local Greeks, far more sophisticated than in most other parts of the country, are swelled by Italians who have made the short sea crossing from the 'heel' of Italy, and by thousands of young British visitors.

For, after Athens, Corfu is the most popular holiday destination in Greece for Britons. A lush, green, and sometimes humid island, it lies just off the Adriatic coast where Greece shares a border with the forbidden land of Albania. Many of the tourists—65 per cent of them British—who arrive in Corfu in the swarms of charter planes which land at the airport every summer afternoon, or who make the ferry crossing from Italy or the mainland Greek port of Igoumenitsa, probably feel that they are visiting an island which is typically Greek. But Corfu can never be said to epitomise Greece.

Although the people are unquestionably Greek, Corfu has more in common with the other countries of the Adriatic than with mainland Greece, and the island's landscape, atmosphere, and manners are western. No doubt this is largely due to Corfu's history, for over the centuries it has been conquered by the Goths, the Romans, the Normans, the Venetians, the Turks, the French, and finally by the British. The fifty years of British rule ended in 1864 when Corfu and the other Ionian islands were finally reunited with Greece, but Britain left behind a legacy in the shape of those two nineteenth-century staples: cricket and ginger beer.

Cricket is still played on the Esplanade Square every summer

Saturday afternoon, and attracts large and appreciative crowds of Corfiotes and visitors alike. The local cricketers even have their 'own' bar in the town, in the corner of a rather smart grocery store, and although they do not always set a very high standard of competition the two local teams are delighted when they are challenged by visiting Naval sides or by the scratch elevens made up every year by organisations like British Airways.

In another piece of ceremonial smacking of the colonial past, the Esplanade resounds on Sunday afternoons to the clamour of a brass band playing on a garishly-painted Victorian bandstand. And in the nearby *tavernas* the favourite non-alcoholic drink is still ginger beer—sweeter and more refreshing than its modern British counterpart, and now known in idiomatic Greek as *tsintsi birra*.

Corfu even has a western European climate, for although the summers are sunny and often stickily warm, the winter months can be very wet and even the National Tourist Organisation of Greece, which is not quick to confess to bad weather, recommends that visitors to the island between November and February should pack a mackintosh and an umbrella. The island benefits from its wet winter, however, by being blessed with a richly green landscape dominated by cypress trees and myriads of olive trees which are said to total three million. Corfiotes, anxious to impress, scoff at this meagre total and insist: 'There are many more than three million olive trees on our island.'

The only other thing that Corfu has in abundance is menfolk with the name of Spyros. They are named after Aghios (St) Spiridon, an import from Cyprus whose mortal remains were smuggled out of Istanbul in a sack and transferred to the glass topped coffin which now reposes in the red-tiled church of St Spiridon in the old Venetian quarter of Corfu Town.

A number of miracles are ascribed to St Spiridon, including the breaking of the siege of Corfu in 1716 when a Greek and Italian force of 5,000 men and a violent storm combined to put paid to the Turkish fleet and an attacking army 30,000 strong. In a rather grisly ritual, the remains of St Spiridon are still paraded triumphantly around the town four times a year, but after 400 years of such treatment the ageing saint is beginning to look badly in need of both a rest and, hopefully, a decent burial.

The Venetian parts of Corfu Town are the most attractive. Although the Venetian citadel which dominates the eastern seafront is still a military establishment, it has been given the vestiges of beauty by allowing the moat or canal, which in fact turns the citadel into an island, to be used as a makeshift marina. There is another fortress on a hillside dominating the harbour, with a fine view over the town. To the north of the modern parts of the town one can also wander for hours through the narrow but attractive streets of the Venetian quarter, where bridges link the houses, ornate balconies catch the evening sun, and tiny vineyards flourish in the corners of walled gardens. One square in the old town hides the seventeenth-century 'Well of Kremasti', which bears the inscription in both Latin and modern English: 'This was made by Antonio Kokkini to help the people. 1699.'

It would be nice if the architectural bequests of British rule were as attractive. Alas, Corfu was governed largely by military gentlemen who were lacking in taste and somewhat over-endowed with a desire for self glorification. The Palace of St Michael and St George, an ugly building which dominates the north side of the Esplanade or Plateia, was built by Sir George Whitmore, the colonel of a British regiment stationed on the island, between 1820 and 1823. It became the residence of the high commissioners, and later the seat of the Ionian Senate. After the departure of the British, the Britannia emblem on the roof was pulled down, leaving the building with a peculiarly cock-eyed appearance, and it is a pity that the palace is now used largely as a museum housing nothing more interesting than a collection of Chinese and Japanese porcelain belonging to the Greek Ministry of Education. Corfiotes loyaly remind the British visitor that Britons brought roads, a hospital, a prison, piped water, and piped sewage to Corfu Town; but they also brought the appallingly ugly Ionian rotunda, near the bandstand, built by Sir Thomas Maitland, the erstwhile British High Commissioner on the island, who was popularly known as 'King Tom' because of his autocratic ways. Living up to his reputation, 'King Tom' built the rotunda in memory of himself.

One of the most elegant spots in Corfu Town is the superb Venetian building housing the Rotary Club and the Corfu Reading Society. The latter was founded in 1846 and is the oldest intellectual society of its kind in Greece. It boasts a collection of 20,000 books on Ionian history and literature, and the fine arts, and these are under the care of the society's secretary, Mr Nondas Stamatopoulos, who speaks perfect English and welcomes serious students and enthusiasts to this unique library.

Another attractive spot is the arcaded west side of the square which dates from the French occupation of the island and is a blatant copy of the Parisian colonnades. This houses souvenir shops, cafes and restaurants, and makes up part of the route of the *volta*. One seldom sees a passing policeman because Corfu Town —in common with Athens and Patras—has its own municipal police force, and in Corfu they prefer to remain as unobtrusive as possible.

One of the traditional sights of Corfu Town is the horse-drawn *monippo* (literally: one horse) carriages, the horses bedecked in brightly-coloured straw hats through which their long dark ears poke absurdly and which somehow contrive to make them look like ageing tarts. Riding in a *monippo* can be an expensive business, and photographing them can be expensive too, for the driver will pursue you with demands for money if he should catch you snapping his horse.

The beautiful villa of Mon Repos, situated in a park overlooking the sea, is another legacy of the British occupation which later became the summer residence of the Greek royal family. Prince Philip was born in the villa, below which is a well-equipped public beach—the best within easy reach of the town. To reach Corfu's many other beaches and beauty spots, visitors will need to rely either upon an expensive taxi or else on the local bus services, which on Sunday becomes erratic and, in some parts of the island, non-existent. Hiring a car is very expensive and this has brought about a mini-boom in the hire of mopeds which cost about one-fifth of the price of a hired car and can be seen puttering their way all over Corfu. Bicycles can also be hired very cheaply.

With steep, stony tracks leading down to many of the beaches, accidents are fairly common among people who are unused to being back on two wheels, and both moped-riders and cyclists often bear the scars of their travels on their knees or elbows. The Corfiotes, now well used to the sound of mopeds toppling on to gravel, can be relied upon to offer instant sympathy and medicaments. But while your arm is being dabbed with a soothing lotion it is worth checking up on what exactly the lotion is. A friend who took a tumble in a tiny village was tended by an ancient crone who muttered unintelligible words of comfort while pouring a sticky brown liquid on to the assortment of cuts and grazes. Smiling toothlessly, the crone then pointed proudly to the label on the bottle, which read: 'Expectorant linctus.' The cuts and grazes, one should add, mended with surprising speed.

South of Corfu Town the road passes through the peaceful landscape of Kanoni; skirts the lagoon of Halikiopoulou which is separated from the sea by a long, narrow causeway; goes past a shorter breakwater which leads to the white convent on a tiny islet; overlooks the cypress-girded chapel on Pondikonisi, or Mouse Island—the subject of tens of thousands of Corfu holiday photographs—and skirts the international airport. Ahead lies the extraordinarily ugly Palace of Achilleon, about twelve miles from the town, which the German Kaiser, Wilhelm II, bought in 1907. Its interior is a monument to bad taste, complete with such oddities as a throne-like lavatory and a desk with a riding saddle as its chair. Outside the main entrance to the palace is a huge marble statue called 'Achilles Wounded', on the pedestal of which the Kaiser had engraved the modest inscription: 'To the greatest of Greeks from the greatest of Germans'. From the attractive wooded grounds it is only a short walk down to the fishing village of Benitses, situated among olive groves and now a popular centre for self-catering villa holidays. Benitses has a good beach, as does the ancient village of Messonghi farther south.

Other excursions include a trip to the promontory of Paleokastritsa, two-thirds of the way up the coast from Corfu Town on a good road built by British troops—ostensibly for military purposes but, according to some reports, constructed principally to help the then High Commissioner, Sir Frederick Adam, and his friends to reach some of the island's more delectable picnic spots. On a headland to the north of the bay there is a Byzantine monastery in a particularly picturesque setting. To the north-east the country becomes rougher, but it is still attractive. At Nissaki a path leads up to the summit of Pantokrator, at 3,000 feet the island's highest peak, from which it is possible to see both the Italian coast to the west and the mountains of Macedonia in the east.

At the far north of the island is another pretty village, Cassiopi, whose attractive little port is being made even more attractive by some imaginative landscaping. The comparatively fast stretch of road back to Corfu Town is particularly interesting, twisting through the valleys and soaring precipitiously round sheer rock faces in its own minor challenge to France's Corniche and Italy's Amalfi Drive. The route is dotted with *tavernas*, and only three miles away—so close that at times you feel you can throw a stone down on to it—lies the coast of Albania.

About halfway between Cassiopi and Corfu is another growing holiday village, Ipsos, on a big sheltered bay which unfortunately has only a narrow shingle beach. For the most part the village's *tavernas* have become untypically noisy and garish, and the service, seldom good anywhere in Greece, can be really awful—with one visitor claiming to have waited a whole three hours before being served.

But there are no such problems in the very un-Greek Pig and Whistle, a strange building to the north of the village which manages to look like a couple of converted nissen huts but which, in fact, contains a restaurant and bar. There, the large and fiercely-moustached proprietor, Andreas, an individualist if ever there was one, serves you if he likes the look of you and ignores you if he does not. Andreas is popular with visiting Britons because of the colourful collection of British tea towels, depicting every conceivable scene from Trooping the Colour to a Scottish croft, which festoon the ceiling of his bar. Despite having three or four helpers, Andreas likes to make out all the restaurant bills, serve all the drinks, and collect all the money himself, so service can again be slow. But the Pig and Whistle is a cheerful, friendly place in which to spend an evening, and it does have the big advantage that you have no doubt about the time at which your evening's festivities will end. Andreas calls 'time' by ringing a bell, blowing a whistle, and shouting 'Goodbye'. Hints don't come any bigger than that.

Service can also be poor in some of the more formal restaurants in Corfu Town, but they do have the advantage of a wider choice on the menus: try the Aigli or the Rex. Prices, however, can be much steeper than in a *taverna*, especially in places where Greek music or dancing is featured.

Hotel standards on Corfu vary, and some of the newer ones cannot be recommended. Prices are related to the grade of hotel, of course, but the grading is not always easy to understand. One cannot fault the Corfu Palace on the edge of town, or the Kontakali Palace, which is said to be the best-run hotel on the island and which does its best to live up to this reputation. I especially like the Grand Hotel Glyfada, on the west coast, which is in a superb if rather remote setting and is run by the Bouas family who own the magnificent Florentine-Renaissance style Hotel Castello, farther north. Both hotels are lavishly furnished with family antiques. But 'B'-grade hotels like the Aeolos Beach, which is used by several inclusive tour operators, also set a high standard. There is an exceptionally helpful branch of the Greek tourist office, E.O.T., on Corfu at Diikitirion, in Corfu Town.

The director, Mr John Tranakas, offered this explanation for the island's popularity with British visitors: 'Not only is our history linked with that of Britain, but there is a large British community here,' he said. 'So it is, in a way, a little bit of home'.

He did not add that it is 'a little bit of home' with hot sunshine, a casual and relaxed air—and all those beautiful girls. What he did add, in a heart-catching farewell, was the same message which implicitly goes to all British holidaymakers: 'I hope you will come back to Corfu soon, to sit in the sun, and drink ginger beer —and perhaps watch the cricket.'

Five other main islands make up the Ionian group: Paxos (with its tiny neighbour Antipaxos), Lefkas, Ithaca, Kefalinia, and Zakinthos. Ithaca and Zakinthos suffered heavy damage during the earthquakes of 1953 and 1958, and because of rebuilding many villages have lost their original charm. But the islands still make up a splendid panorama when seen from the sea, and there is an indefinable romance about sailing in the waters of Ulysses.

Paxos, with its profusion of lush green vegetation, has an almost tropical appearance, and its isolated beaches—frequented by seals but seldom by people—make it an ideal get-away-from-it-all destination. Modern bungalows can be rented on the island, and transport is by *caique* from Corfu. Antipaxos is the retirement home of several Britons, and equally quiet.

Lefkas, between Paxos and the southern trio of islands, only just qualifies as an island, for it is separated from the Greek mainland only by a marshy isthmus and a canal. But it does have the individuality of an island, and the annual festival of art and literature in August has proved a big attraction. The island is reached by a chain ferry linking causeways on the mainland and on Lefkas, and one's first impression is a feeling of disappointment, for it is not as beautiful a spot as guidebooks and pamphlets suggest. Once again, earthquake damage—this time in 1958—is to blame, for many of the island's man-made beauties were spoiled, including a lot of property in the Turkish-style town. Unfortunately, the local residents have not helped matters by making repairs to their close-packed timber-framed houses with chunks of corrugated iron, and the open drains can only add to the visitor's distaste.

Fortunately, the works forged by a mightier hand than man's are still attractive, and the glorious 13-mile coastal drive to the Bay of Vliko confirms this. En route, at Nidrion, there are rooms to let in the houses above the steeply-shelving pebble beach, and a good grillhouse. There is also a fine view of the small islands scattered between Lefkas and Ithaca, which include the well-guarded private family island of Skorpios, where shipping magnate Aristotle Onassis married Mrs Jackie Kennedy in 1968 and was buried in 1975. The island is so secret that it does not even appear on some local maps, but the fishermen of Lefkas, cashing in on curiosity, will take visitors around 'the Onassis island' fairly cheaply.

Beyond Vliko the roads are badly signposted, and it is hard to find one's way. The tenacious will reach the vast, empty, sandy beaches around places like Sivota (where a little restaurant specialises in fresh lobster), and Vassiliki (where the price of a bed for the night in a private house bedecked with a flower-filled balcony is so cheap as to be laughable). A romantic spot, in the true sense of the word, is the Leap of Lefkas, where the paths of criminals and lovers once crossed. The criminals had to leap into the sea from the clifftop in order to prove their innocence; the lovers traditionally made the leap to cure unrequited love and, as the poetess Sappho is said to have discovered, the cure was often permanent—for the cliff is 236 feet high.

To lovers of the Odyssey, Ithaca can be a disappointment. But Homer did warn us: 'A precipitous isle, unfit for horses . . . poor for goats. . . .' It is not too good for holidaymakers either, although the principal port of Vathi might be worth a visit as well as the archaeological sites and the various spots identified, sometimes on rather dubious grounds, as the settings for various scenes from the Homeric legends.

A natural channel, in places not much more than a mile wide, separates Ithaca from Kefalinia which is, in fact, the largest of the Ionian islands and can rival even Corfu for the variety and beauty of its scenery. The port, and capital, of Argostoli is a surprisingly modern town, having been rebuilt after suffering almost total destruction in 1953. It lies on one side of the long, deep, fjord-like Livadi Bay which splits the island into two uneven parts. There are good sandy beaches at Platis Gialos, just outside Argostoli, and across the bay at Lixourion, the island's second city. Yachting facilities are also good.

Of special interest is the village of Kastro, which stands among the ruins of churches, monasteries, and houses; the medieval village of San Giorgio which once held 15,000 inhabitants inside its hefty ramparts; and, across the Plain of Krane, the picturesque village of Assos. At Mazarakata, excavations at a number of Mycenaean tombs have produced a haul of beautiful vases. Ferry services link Patras with the little port of Sami, nestling beneath a Venetian castle and overlooking Ithaca on the opposite side of the island to Argostoli.

Farther south still, off the coast of the Peloponnese opposite Kilini, lies Zakinthos, which is also known as Zante and which, like Corfu, boasts a mild climate and soft scenery dotted with vineyards and olive groves—a combination which moved the Venetians to christen the island 'the Flower of the Levant'. But Zakinthos also suffered heavily in the 1953 earthquake, and the modern buildings now scattered over the island seem to intrude upon the scenery rather than melting into it.

This criticism does not strictly apply to the main town, called Zakinthos too, where rebuilding has been in a modified version of the original Venetian—the houses and spacious squares somehow reminding one of Rhodes Town. There are several good, modern hotels, and the charges for accommodation are very low. The ferry boat *Proteus* makes several daily crossings to Kilini.

For a comparatively remote island, Zakinthos is remarkably alert to the demands of the tourist trade. In the town the seafront is lined with cinemas, one of them showing English-language films during the summer and employing touts who enquire anxiously of visitors: 'Are you going to the English movie tonight?' Near the top of the hill dominating the harbour is the Church of St Nicholas, which boasts a fine silver-framed, life-size, gold icon of the Virgin and Child, dating from 840. Restaurants in town are good and English is spoken in many of them; the surprising local speciality is goulash, and there is a good local wine which costs less than many soft drinks.

Roads in the north-west of Zakinthos vary from the bad to the non-existent, but it is worth hiring a local boatman to take you to the 'Blue Grotto' caves. To the south there are good beaches, often backed by *tavernas* specialising in delicious red mullet. Spear fishing is good from many of the island's beaches. And, like Corfu, Zakinthos is an island which tugs at the heart-strings; despite the frequency of the ferry services, it seems as though the whole town turns out to wave you goodbye and to call: '*Kalo taxithi*'. It means: safe journey.

10. The Cyclades Islands

As the day lengthened, so did the estimates of the time at which our ferry would arrive at the strange, volcanic island of Santorini. 'You will arrive at about 8 p.m.,' said the man in the booking office in Athens. 'We will be there at about half-past ten tonight,' said the crewman who brought round cold drinks just after the ship had sailed from Piraeus. 'I think we will dock at about midnight,' said Captain Dimitrios over a large and somewhat untypical Greek lunch of spaghetti.

Not that it mattered very much. The good ship *Evangelistria*, a vessel of mixed parentage which claimed a British corvette among its antecedents, ploughed steadily through the Aegean among the Cyclades—the beautiful cluster of islands to the south-east of the mainland of Greece—all day at a top speed of 14 knots. The sun shone, and there was hardly a ripple on the water.

Islands came and went; islands like Siros, once the capital of the Cyclades and the place which claims to have produced even more of Greece's wealthy shipowners than its rivals in the Dodecanese group of islands. The *Evangelistria* tied up briefly at the little port and capital of Siros, Ermoupoulis, where clusters of white houses tumble down to the sea and hawkers will offer you boxes of the produce for which the island is famous: Turkish Delight as delicious as anything that ever came out of Turkey.

14 Kos: the former mosque in the town centre

'We will stay here for ten minutes,' said Captain Dimitrios. Despite the haphazard nature of the ferry timetables in this part of the world, he was as good as his word—and three bearded youths who had decided to take the risk and do some shopping were left, waving desperately, on the quayside. As they receded into the distance the captain obviously felt that some words of comfort were called for and, stepping briefly out of the wheelhouse, he called after them politely: 'There is another boat tomorrow.'

Eventually, the clatter of the anchor chain awoke me at 3.30 a.m. There is another, more accessible, anchorage on Santorini, but most ferry boats—and all cruise liners—choose to moor at the foot of the cliff below the island's capital, Fira. There can hardly be a more dramatic landing place in the entire Mediterranean, and getting to the top of the cliff constitutes an adventure in itself. First, clutching your luggage, you have to clamber down into the tenders which ferry passengers ashore from the bigger vessels. Then, at the harbourside, donkeys and mules wait to carry you and your cases up the 587 steps—numbered in case anyone should disbelieve the tally—to the town itself. You haven't ridden on a donkey or a mule before? Nor have most of the other Western European and American visitors to the island, but it is not as hard as it looks and there is no other way to reach the top—especially if, like me, you arrive in the middle of the night.

Arriving at such an hour means that it is not until next morning that one appreciates what you, and the donkey, have achieved in reaching the top; you have climbed the crater of a volcano. For Santorini is just that: the tip of a vast underwater volcano, 37 miles across, the edge of which has crumbled to let in the sea. The huge circular bay in which the ships moor is in fact the very heart of the volcano, and it is far from extinct. Although the water is many hundreds of feet deep, the strange, black island of Nea Kaimene arose in the centre of the bay between 1711 and

15 Rhodes: the gate on the west side of the old town

1712, and a sister island disappeared in 1868. There have been frequent earthquakes, the most recent in 1956 when half the buildings on the west coast were destroyed.

It is this tumultuous past which has made people suspect that Santorini is all that remains of the lost 'continent' of Atlantis. These claims have been given weight both by the fractured collection of historical facts and other evidence referred to in Chapter 1, and by the work of Professor Spiros Marinatos, of the Athens Academy, who until his recent death was in charge of the archaeological excavations at Akrotiri, on the southernmost promontory of Santorini, where since 1967 a Bronze Age town of some 30,000 inhabitants has been slowly dug out of the pumice. Whole streets of two and three-storey houses, many with staircases and the remains of wooden door and window frames, have come to light and now shelter under a vast roof of corrugated iron. In archaeological terms, however, investigations have only just begun, and there are indications that Akrotiri may soon rival even Knossos, on nearby Crete, both in size and interest.

Fira itself is a pretty town of white houses clinging to the edge of the cliff and tiny blue-domed churches which look as though they are made of icing sugar. The view over Santorini and its neighbouring islands is superb, and for much of the year the area is bathed in the sparkingly clear sunshine peculiar to the Aegean. There are a couple of hotels of which the Atlantis is the best, but many houses in the town and in outlying districts offer accommodation. Except in the hotels, the food is the usual *taverna* fare and not always as good as in many other parts of Greece. To drink there are the famous Santorini white and rosé wines, which taste like the home-made wines that they are but carry a compensatory kick; beware of ordering them in hotel restaurants, however, because there is a price mark-up of more than 100 per cent.

As well as Akrotiri, it is important not to miss Kamari Beach—composed of black, volcanic sand which makes every other colour, from fishermen's nets to visitors' bathing costumes, look extraordinarily bright. There is an erratic bus service to the beach from Fira, but the bus is worth waiting for because the fare is only about one-twentieth of what the mercenary local taxi drivers will charge you. But the most fascinating excursion of all is the 20-minute boat trip to Nea Kaimene, a stunted, evil-looking island of black rocks and volcanic ash and with only a few tufts of grass and one solitary bush growing on it. From the landing stage it is a half-hour climb up to the Metaxa Crater, which is still active. Blasts of heat still pant from the fissures in the rocks, staining the ground a sulphurous yellow and giving the crater the distinctive smell of a child's chemistry set.

In many ways, it is a relief to escape back to the light and lushness of Santorini, and to make the now familiar climb to the top of the cliff on the broad back of a mule which contains, according to local legend, the soul of a sinner serving out his time in purgatory. The 587 steps are certainly an awesome punishment, but instead of thoughts of repentance the steep climb (impossible on foot if you have any luggage) brings only a sense of wonder as the view unfolds once again. Santorini has recently reverted to its ancient name of Thira, and at present both are in use to the bewilderment of locals and tourists alike. The problem could be settled by readopting the third name by which Santorini was once known: 'Kallisti', which means—appropriately enough—'most beautiful'.

And yet, all of the 39 islands in the Cyclades group are beautiful, and if Santorini is a personal favourite it is because it manages to combine the traditional peace and tranquillity of the Cyclades with dramatic scenery and a past history which can be the subject for endless speculation and conjecture. Apart from when a cruise ship calls, it is also free of the crowds which have ruined islands like Mykonos.

The ancient Greeks called the Cyclades 'the wheeling ones', for they seemed to form a circle around the sacred island of Delos. Today, more prosaically, the islands are divided into three groups—Eastern, Central, and Western—and only 24 of them are inhabited. In this latter respect the smaller islands contrast greatly with Mykonos, the most popular of the Cyclades and the island around which tourism in the area revolves. In summer, Mykonos is the place which beckons holidaymakers in Greece to the Cyclades; the place which becomes everybody's 'typical Greek island'. Its narrow streets are jammed with youngsters wearing a minimum of clothes and making a maximum of noise, and even some of the tiny shops have found it worthwhile to turn themselves into western-style boutiques.

In spring especially, however, Mykonos is still worth seeing, for it is then uncrowned and it does epitomise the Cyclades group —if anything can be said to epitomise 39 vastly differing islands—in several important respects.

Mykonos, alleged by mythology to be the burial place of the Centaurs, was an infamous pirate base as recently as the eighteenth century, but the islanders put their ships to more lawful use during the nineteenth-century struggles for Greek independence and today they are proud of their nautical tradition—as are most of the people of the Aegean. But the men of Mykonos have matched their adventures at sea with the endeavours that they have put into turning their bare, stony island, which is perpetually short of water, into a productive place; every possible scrap of land is cultivated, and every possible source of energy has been put to work. Even the graceful windmills which typify the island still turn lazily all summer long.

The result is delightful, for Mykonos presents a picture of an island which is truly treasured by its people. The whitewashed houses, built in the typical style of the islands, are warmed by orange shutters, picturesque wooden balconies, and countless pots full of flowers. The tiny churches—360 of them, on an island of less than 4,000 people—are typically Greek. And the beaches, clean and still relatively unspoilt, are perfect for both water skiing and for underwater fishing.

The two most famous beaches are Megali Ammos and St Stephen's, which have bars and refreshment facilities (try *amygdalota*, the almond paste of the island) and a cosmopolitan clientèle. There is also a fine archaeological museum on Mykonos, containing many of the finds made on neighbouring Delos: eighth-century-BC geometric Cycladic vases, funeral vases of lead and marble, Roman statues, jewellery, and household articles. The museum makes a good introduction to Delos itself.

After a siesta at the hotel (try the first-class Leto), many people like to shop in the maze of lanes and alleyways behind the compact waterfront in the town of Mykonos, where dresses made in Mykonos fabrics, and other articles of local handicrafts can be found as well as the more usual tourist souvenirs. And as the last rays of the sun strike gold off the compact houses which give the town—and the island—its individuality, it is time to think of dinner. Like all international resorts, Mykonos has its western-style restaurants, its discos, and round-the-clock 'nightclubs', but you will fare just as well and far more cheaply in one of the *tavernas* near the waterfront, where you will hear *bouzouki* music (and, if you are lucky, hear the songs and see the dances of the local fishermen), and eat the specialities of the island: lobster, shrimp, roast sucking pig, *louza* sausage, and peppery *kopanisti* cheese.

Just a day on Mykonos can convey the island's air of timelessness. But if Mykonos is timeless, then the island opposite, Delos, is more so. A small, rocky piece of land, not much more than three miles long and half a mile wide, Delos was once the religious centre of the Aegean, and seeing it is still one of the highlights of any visit to the Cyclades.

Greek legend, ever inventive, says that Delos was once a floating island on which Leto, a mortal who had taken Zeus as a lover, sought refuge from the jealous and vengeful Hera. Zeus helpfully caused the island to take anchor at the spot where it rests today, and there Leto gave birth to Apollo. Be that as it may Delos, the 'island of light', was a religious, artistic and commercial centre of the ancient Greek and Roman worlds, and the island—with its famous marble lions—is now a tourist centre.

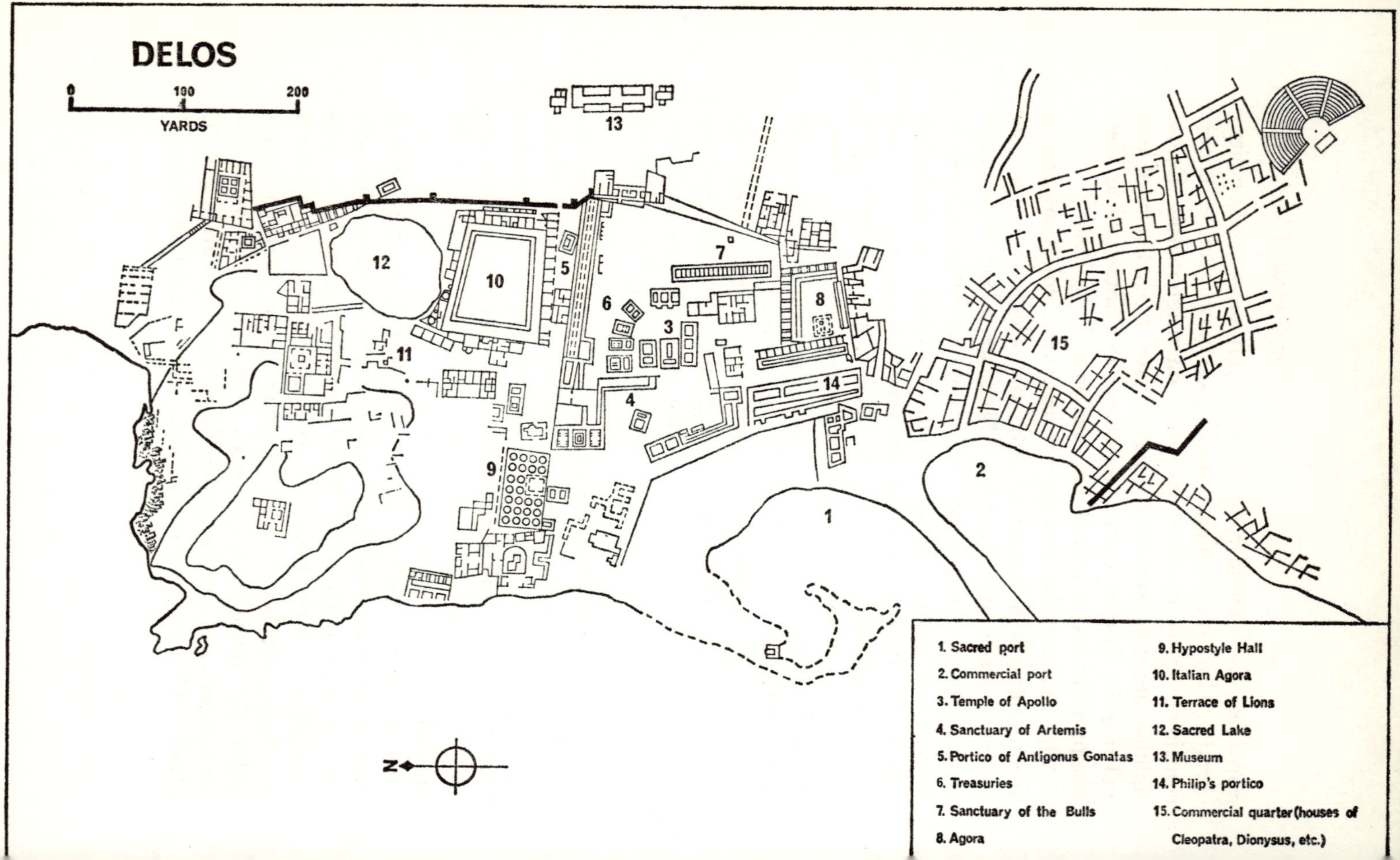
DELOS
0
100
200
YARDS
N
1
2
3
4
5
6
7
8
9
10
11
12
13
14
15
1. Sacred port
2. Commercial port
3. Temple of Apollo
4. Sanctuary of Artemis
5. Portico of Antigonus Gonatas
6. Treasuries
7. Sanctuary of the Bulls
8. Agora
9. Hypostyle Hall
10. Italian Agora
11. Terrace of Lions
12. Sacred Lake
13. Museum
14. Philip's portico
15. Commercial quarter (houses of Cleopatra, Dionysus, etc.)

Travelling by *caique* from Mykonos, it takes about an hour to reach Delos. Because Delos was sacred, birth and death were not allowed to occur there—and the *caique* passes Rheneia, where pregnant women and the old and sick were taken, on its way to Delos. Ahead lies Delos itself, with its safe, natural harbour, and crowned by its sacred mountain, the conical, rocky, 386-feet-high Kinthos. The natural harbour and the legend of Apollo made Delos important to the ancient Greeks, who ranked it with Delphi, Olympia and Epidaurus as a sanctuary. Choirs of young virgins appeared there at the annual religious festivities (a tribute which must have particularly pleased the rapacious Zeus), and during the Athenian ascendancy pilgrims arrived in Delos from all over the known world to see the processions and games, or to consult the oracle. The island developed into a city, full of temples and grand houses, and it reached its peak when the Romans granted it tax concessions which enabled it to develop as a trading centre between East and West.

The glory did not last. As the Roman Empire broke up, so Delos became the centre of a struggle that rolled back and forth across the island. The islanders fled, or were slaughtered, and the great buildings were demolished. The pirates moved in to make it a base, and scavengers from other islands looted it for building materials. It was not until 1873 that excavations began to uncover ancient Delos once again—and these excavations continue to this day.

One needs three hours, and a detailed guide book, to tour the ruins of Delos properly. The Sacred Harbour, the Sanctuary, and the Gymnasium are beautifully preserved, as is the Sacred Way and a number of temples and shrines. After a while one loses count of the wall paintings, the mosaics, and the fallen pieces of sculpture. But the marble lions guarding the regal avenue which divides the island are something one does not miss, or forget. You can stay in the tourist pavilion, but perhaps Delos, with its lions gazing blindly out across the Aegean, are something to see and then leave behind. Sad, lovely Delos has had its moment of glory . . . and one could almost wish that it was time for the island to pull up its anchors, and sail away once more.

After Santorini and Delos, it is easy to think of the Cyclades Islands as some vast archaeological site—and so, in a way, they are. This is where Greece began. But for thousands of holidaymakers these islands are a place in which it is possible to get away from it all, a place in which it is possible to relax, explore, move on, and finally settle wherever happens to take your fancy.

The Cyclades are served by almost daily ferry services from Athens, with *caique* connections to the smaller islands. These ferries are very cheap, especially for those prepared to travel 'deck class', but as I have explained earlier in this chapter the services are erratic, and anyone with a flight to catch in Athens should leave two or three days for a journey which should not take more than six or seven hours.

The reason is that the ferries are mostly privately owned, and operate on circular routes, which can be changed according to the whim of captain or owner. What is worse, they also tend to ignore one another's existence. Ask on the quayside at Santorini when the next ferry leaves for Athens, and you may well be told: 'The day after tomorrow.' Then, when you reach the top of the cliff, you may see a ferry boat sail in, set down a few passengers, and set sail again in the direction of Athens. What the ferry man on the quayside was in fact telling you was that *his* particular shipping line's next ferry to Athens is the day after tomorrow. The only day on which there are no such problems is Sunday, when there are no ferry services at all.

All this gives an island-hopping holiday an air of uncertainty which is infuriating if you are in a hurry and very relaxing and amusing if you aren't. The only thing that you can be reasonably certain of is that the ferry will leave Athens on time, for reasons of prestige. After that, you are in the hands of men like Captain Dimitrios.

The first island of any importance that one is likely to see is Kea, only 12 miles off Cape Sounion and another notorious pirate hideout in the not-too-distant past. The only raiders that it attracts today are the spear fishermen for whom it is ideal, but it also has quiet beaches, particularly on the north-west shore, and a peaceful atmosphere. The islanders produce a dark red wine, honey, and delicious apricot jelly.

Next, in the Western group of islands, comes Kythnos, the original city-state, another peaceful spot given over to the rearing of sheep and goats. Loutra, one of the three villages, is the only thermal resort in the Cyclades, and its spring waters are supposed to bring relief to sufferers from rheumatism and arthritis as well as developing resistance against the chills of the winter to come. There are four good beaches, but visitors usually want to devote their time to watching one of the popular local festivals, based on pagan rites. The Eastern celebrations (which are *not* pagan, but purely religious) are unforgettable.

Serifos is a barren-looking island, which the Romans used for exiling troublemakers, but the Taxiarchon Monastery has a library of rare Byzantine manuscripts and there is a tenth-century Byzantine church in the village of Panaghia. Local celebrations are again picturesque. But if stark Serifos is a place for the purist, perhaps the next island, Sifnos, is for the sun-seeker—for the huge stretch of sands at Plati Yalo (literally: 'broad shore') are the longest in the Cyclades and show every sign of becoming a tourist centre. Gold and silver were once mined on Sifnos, and a wealthy past is apparent in the abundance of relics: temples, medieval churches, and a ruined Venetian castle. There are pottery workshops in the harbour of Kamares, Byzantine treasures in the cathedral in Apollonia, and a swinging night-life in the holiday centre of Artemona, a pretty village dotted with windmills.

'Kimolia' in Greek means chalk, so it can easily be guessed how the bleached island of Kimolos got its name. The famous pirate Barbarossa made his headquarters on Kimolos, but today it is a very quiet spot with good beaches and several important archaeological sites. Tourist interest is mostly concentrated on adjacent Milos, which is where the famous statue of the Venus de Milo was discovered and from which, the islanders will remind you accusingly, it was removed to the Louvre in Paris. Milos is a horseshoe-shaped island, with its port, Adamanda, near the bottom of the crescent. The most important excavations are at Phylakopi, where traces of three successive cities have been uncovered dating from the early Minoan period, and there are several fine beaches including the one at Hivadolimni, which is well-known for its sea-food.

Besides Siros, the administrative capital of the Cyclades, the Central group of islands is dominated by Paros, its small neighbour of Antiparos, and Naxos. Paros—once inhabited by Cretans and known as Minoa—is famous as a source of marble but is now becoming well-known for its excellent beaches. The main town, Parikia, offers a panorama of windmills, orchards, and olive groves, and the monastery church of Panaghia Ekatontapiliani contains a Byzantine museum. There are good beaches at Aliki and Drys, near the town, and at Marpissa on the other side of the island. Quiet Antiparos, usually visited on day-trips from Paros, has a stalactite-filled cave on the Hill of St John.

Naxos, the largest of the Cyclades group, is also famous for marble and for having been conquered by Barbarossa. Unfinished statutes have been left lying at Flerio and Apollona, sad reminders of the part that the quarries of Naxos played an important part in the development of classic art. Now this island, which great empires fought over, is a holiday playground; and its roads, accommodation, beaches and fishing are all good. There are attractive *tavernas* at Komiaki Sangri, and folk dancing in the main square at Kinidari.

Beyond Paros and Naxos a sickle-shaped curve of smaller islands bar the way to Santorini: Amorgos, with its precious Byzantine icons and manuscripts and a fountain in the Church of St George which has always been regarded as an oracle; hospitable Ios, said to be the burial place of Homer, with its very typical Cyclades landscape and atmosphere; remote Sikinos; and rocky

Pholegandros. Santorini itself has a small neighbour in the shape of Anafi, the most southerly island of the Cyclades group, which mythology says rose from the sea on the orders of Apollo to give shelter to the storm-bound Argonauts. Archaeological sites on the island bear traces of the Apollo cult, in another of those strange links between fact and fiction that the Greek past throws up.

Finally there are the Eastern islands of Andros, Tinos, and Mykonos. Wooded, hilly Andros, with sylvan scenery quite untypical of the area, is the second largest of the Cyclades islands and has a thriving fruit-growing industry. It is dominated by an immense Venetian fortress, and is developing a number of holiday resorts along its fine beaches. These resorts include Korthion, Palcopolis (which also has some archaeological remains), and Sarisa—a village which also produces mineral water from a local spring.

Tinos already has good hotel accommodation and all the trappings of a tourist infrastructure—but it is not the beaches that are the attraction. For Tinos is the 'Lourdes of the Aegean', a place of pilgrimage which has sprung up around the contents of the white marble cathedral, Panaghia Evangelistria, dominating the town. Inside the cathedral is a jewel-studded icon discovered in 1822 and said to be capable of working miracles. Pilgrims flock to the island on 15 August every year—and as a result Tinos is a place for the tourist to avoid.

The other islands should not be avoided. Indeed, they should not be missed. For, whatever the drawbacks as far as transport is concerned, the Cyclades offer all the delights of island-hopping with the comforts of proper accommodation and a varied diet. Cool winds temper the summer sun, and that peculiar light brings a glow to the islands.

And even if you cannot persuade the captain of your particular ferry boat to hazard a guess as to what time you might arrive at the island of your choice, it doesn't matter. It is enough to know that you *will* arrive, and that the islands are there for the taking.

11. Rhodes and the Dodecanese Islands

The little man in the minibus was enthusiastic. 'Come and see the night life of Rhodes,' he appealed to prospective customers at the hotel. 'You will find it very exciting.'

To be fair, he did try to make it exciting. But night life is hard to find on a damp autumn evening in Rhodes—the Crusaders' isle which now belongs to Greece and which hangs like a jewel off the Turkish coast. There was a meal (served with unusual speed) in a *taverna*, an energetic but somewhat confused exhibition of Greek dancing, a quick drive around the darkened city of Rhodes, and a visit to an otherwise empty nightclub. Long before midnight most of the little man's customers had decided to settle for an early night rather than a riotous one.

For Rhodes, the largest of the Dodecanese islands, is essentially a sunshine resort—and although the islanders try hard to keep the growing numbers of winter package holidaymakers amused, there really is not much to do when the sun disappears.

Fortunately it does not disappear very often, and even in winter the climate is mild. In summer, Rhodes is the holiday choice of many Greeks: one in every six of the island's visitors is a Greek, although this popularity must be partly due to the fact that Rhodes and the other twelve Dodecanese islands are a duty-free area.

'Most people come here for the sun,' says Nondas Solounias,

president of the island's Hotel Owners' Association. 'In summer you can tell how long people have been in Rhodes by the colour of their skin. People who have been here for ten days get browner than islanders get in the whole summer.'

It is a fitting tribute to an island reputed to have been the home of Helios, the sun god. Helios was commemorated in about 290 BC by one of the best-known but most mysterious of the Seven Wonders of the Ancient World, the Colossus of Rhodes, a giant 90-feet statue said to have straddled the old harbour entrance. The bronze statue collapsed in an earthquake after about 75 years, and today nothing more dramatic than a row of silent windmills at the water's edge greets visitors arriving by *caique* at the Mandraki port. For those arriving by air there is a hazard in the shape of two steep hills, one on either side of the airport, which in certain conditions (usually in winter) create an upward draught making it impossible to land. The island authorities are now building a new airport which it is hoped will alleviate the problem.

Rhodes Town occupies the northernmost tip of the 77-km-long, lozenge-shaped island. Because of its important strategic position, Rhodes has been overrun by a succession of Mediterranean conquerors. The Dorians, arriving from mainland Greece, built Lindos; the Romans, arriving from Italy, were the first to use Rhodes as a tourist resort, and both Cicero and Caesar are said to have liked to holiday on the island. In the Middle Ages the battles between the Saracens and the Crusaders raged around Rhodes, with both sides having possession of it at one time or another. A military order, the Knights of the Order of St John of Jerusalem, turned it into a stronghold. And finally the Turks took the island and held it until 1912, when the Italians took over. Rhodes was incorporated into Greece in 1948.

This rich and varied history is amply illustrated by the wealth of monuments inside the massive, turreted walls of the Old Town.

From the great harbour, where cruise ships and mainland ferries tie up, the famous Street of the Knights passes the cloistered

Hospital of the Knights, now an archaeological museum and containing a noteworthy 2,000-year-old statue of Aphrodite kneeling, and climbs steeply past the Inns of the Seven Tongues into which the Order was divided. In each of these two-storeyed Inns, identified by coats-of-arms outside, lived the knights belonging to a specific Tongue, or language: France, Provence, Auvergne, Spain, Germany, Italy, and England. The fifteenth-century Inn of the Tongue of Auvergne, restored after the First World War and now an arts centre, is a fine example of these Inns. Farther up the hill is the entrance to the Palace of the Grand Masters of the Order of St John, built in the fourteenth century as a fortress within a fortified city and apparently unharmed by the Turkish siege of 1522, but devastated by an explosion in 1856 when the Turks were using it as a prison. It was entirely rebuilt by the Italians during their occupation between the two world wars, with the intention of using it as a royal residence. Inside there is now an interesting collection of ancient mosaics and statues from the island of Kos.

The medieval city walls are among the most impressive in the world, dotted with towers and bastions and surrounded by a dry moat crossed by bridges leading to the three main gateways. Each sector of the walls was defended by one of the Tongues, and visitors can follow in the footsteps of the knights on Tuesday and Saturday afternoons, when there are conducted tours of the ramparts.

The remainder of the Old City within the walls is a maze of picturesque little streets and alleys, dotted with shops, and broken up by pretty fountains and by tiny churches mostly converted into mosques during the centuries of Turkish domination. Turkish influence is still strong in the market-place atmosphere which prevails. Buildings of note are the Castellan's Palace, the Knights' commercial court which the Turks converted into a fish market but which has now been beautifully restored; and the Mosque of Suleiman.

Perhaps because it manages to combine ancient and modern

so gracefully, to say nothing of combining many cultures and influences, Rhodes Town is one of the most attractive cities in Greece. The new town, with its hotels, restaurants and shops, contrasts happily with the old, and both the public parks and the fact that the sea is on three sides of the town give it an unusual spaciousness.

Some of the hotel designs are futuristic. The Rodos Bay Hotel, outside the town, is built up against a mountainside and has its swimming pool on the roof—a combination which gives it the appearance of something out of a James Bond film set. The Plaza is a good 'B'-grade hotel, and even in so sophisticated an island it is still possible to find accommodation in private houses at about £1 a night.

There are marvellous walks, beaches, and excursion sites within easy reach of Rhodes Town. The Moorish-style seaside resort of Kalithea, eight miles out of town, is the spa to which Hippocrates used to send the more affluent of his patients, and even today the waters are recommended for obesity, arthritis, diabetes, and high blood pressure. On the hilltop of Philerimos, approached through a pine forest, one can wander through the ruins of the third-century-BC Temple of Athena and a small Byzantine church. The subterranean Church of Our Lady of Philerimos, with its fifteenth-century frescoes, is close to a small monastery. From the hill a 15-minute walk leads to the famous Doric Fountain on the site of ancient Ialyssos, one of the three cities which the Dorians built on the island.

The second ancient city, Kamiros, known as the 'Pompeii of Rhodes', is about 25 miles out of town on the west coast of the island. Built on the slopes of a hill, it has the remains of a Doric theatre sweeping down to the sea, and is one of the most beautiful spots in Rhodes. But it is its rival, Lindos, on the east coast and about 35 miles from town, which draws the biggest crowds.

Lovely Lindos is, perhaps, everything that a classical site should be. As attractive as the Temple of Sounion, and with an acropolis comparable in richness to that of Athens, it makes a dramatic landmark whether one approaches it by land or sea, with the ruins of the Temple of Athena Lindia catching the sun from their bold position on the promontory of Mount Mamari. The history of Rhodes is encapsulated at Lindos, for one can find the works of Byzantines and Crusaders among the ruins, as well as its Turkish fortifications.

Once separating two harbours, and today dividing two attractive and popular beaches, Lindos is said to have been founded by the apparently indefatiguable Danaos and his family of 50 sons and 50 daughters after they had fled from Egypt. Certainly the site was occupied before the year 2000 BC, and Lindos later became the most important city on the island with its adventurous people venturing abroad to found colonies near present-day Naples and in Sicily. St Paul is believed to have landed at a bay beside Lindos on his way to Rome.

Today Lindos is a pretty village of 650 people, its white houses tumbling down the hillside towards a more modern area, and its streets and courtyards pebbled with tiny black and white stones laid out in patterns. Here shopkeepers beckon passers-by into their spotless showrooms, to sell Greek pottery and handicrafts, and this twentieth-century trade goes on amid surroundings where the Byzantines and the Crusaders both built churches (the latter can still be visited), and where history has left a peculiar air of timelessness.

Beyond Lindos, the road quickly deteriorates, and it is true to say that the southern half of Rhodes is seldom visited by tourists. You will need a hired car to reach this area, but you will be rewarded by remote and empty beaches. If you do not intend to explore these solitary areas there is good transport to be found by bus and excursion coach, and very good beaches close to the town.

Apart from Lindos, the most popular excursion on Rhodes is

16 Crete: the church of Panaghia Kera at Kritsa

to the Valley of the Butterflies, a long, wooded gorge below the 2,000-feet-high mountain retreat of Prophitis Elias, 31 miles from Rhodes Town. In summer, countless golden moths settle on the trees, and at first they are almost invisible because of their colouring. But shake the trees, and a cloud of moths will fill the air like an amber snowstorm. It is a unique and unforgettable sight which, unfortunately, can seldom be captured satisfactorily by the camera.

Because of its beauty Rhodes, the capital of the Dodecanese islands, is known as the 'island of flowers', and in this respect it differs from many of its neighbours, which verge on bleakness. Although tourists do now visit the smaller islands, travelling by *caique* and living in the islanders' homes or in *tavernas*, the Dodecanese as a whole remain the least-known part of Greece to the outside world. The larger islands are developing a tourist infrastructure, with hotels or bungalow complexes, a variety of recreation and entertainment facilities, and ferry services to and from the mainland; but in the smaller islands strung off the Turkish coast the visitor will have no choice but to live as the islanders do, and create his or her own entertainment.

Gaunt, parched Patmos, 106 miles north of Rhodes, perhaps epitomises the other islands adjacent to the coast of Asia Minor, for although it has little to commend it beyond its blue skies and even bluer sea, it is a peaceful spot. It has an important place in history too, for in a bleak, purple porphyry cave, halfway up a hillside, known today as the Cave of the Apocalypse, St John wrote the *Revelations*.

One cannot help seeing the island's other principal attraction, for it is impossible to miss: a monastery which, with its towers and battlements, looks more like a Norman castle than a religious institution. The monastery dominates the whole island, contains some priceless manuscripts and other treasures—including three

17 *Crete: the north aisle of the church of Panaghia Kera*

paintings said to be by St Luke—and has superb views all round Patmos and across to Samos and Ikaria, which are best seen in the dawn light.

Just south of Patmos is Leros, its green valleys and vineyards separated from each other by rocky hills. There are two big bays, Gournas and Porto Lago, one on each side of the island, and on the north-west coast there is good bathing at the two seaside villages, where you can eat fresh sea-food in the *tavernas* of an evening.

Leros and neighbouring Kalymnos are the centre of the Greek sponge-fishing industry, and mountainous Kalymnos is particularly delightful because of its clear blue seas and the ancient traditions which the sponge fishermen have preserved. There are special celebrations when the fishermen set off on their sponge-diving voyages just after Easter, and even more special celebrations when they return again five months later.

Kos, just off the coast of Turkey and a strangely elongated island, is the island of Hippocrates, the father of modern medicine. Hippocrates studied and taught on the island, and there is a huge fourth-century-BC statue of him in the museum of Kos. Islanders will also point out an elderly plane tree in the town, which they claim was planted by Hippocrates despite the fact that a plane tree seldom lives for more than 500 years. There is an imposing castle, and several early Christian and Byzantine churches, to see, as well as a number of attractive villages which can be reached by bus, mule, or bicycle. The islanders will happily hire you a bicycle, which is a popular way of getting around on Kos; as it is a mountainous island, no doubt cycling is also very healthy.

Between Kos and Rhodes are a cluster of four small islands which lack any tourist amenities but make up for this by offering crowd-free beaches and extremely cheap accommodation and meals. They are Simi, praised by the ancients for its beauty; Halki, with just two tiny villages on it; Tilos, which used to produce famous perfumes; and Nisiros, a spa resort. One of the smallest, and certainly the most remote, of the Dodecanese islands is Kastelorizon, just off the coast of Turkey and with a population of only 500. Castel Rosso, the red fortress which gave the island its name, is on top of a reddish-brown hill overlooking the village, and besides the castle it is worth visiting the remarkable Fokiali Caves. There is no hotel, but the islanders will be glad to put up visitors in their spotless homes and the beaches make excellent camping sites.

All of the islands mentioned so far hug the Turkish coast, but three islands farther out into the Aegean are also included in the Dodecanese group. These are Astipalea, halfway between Rhodes and the Cyclades group of islands, and Karpathos and Kasos which are halfway between Rhodes and Crete.

Astipalea was once known as the 'island of fish', and lies in deep fishing waters. But it is now famous for its delicious honey. It is a pretty but seldom-visited island, with a village of white houses distinguished by wooden trelliswork balconies, a number of windmills, a castle, and the big, rocky Maltezana Bay. Although it is officially part of the Dodecanese, Astipalea resembles the Cyclades islands in character, and is perhaps the misplaced thirteenth isle.

Beautiful Karpathos has a dual personality which may yet turn the island into a holiday resort in its own right. The southern part is covered with dense forests and cascading streams—a most un-Grecian style of scenery which acts as a backdrop for fine but deserted beaches. The houses on Karpathos are painted in the traditional style of the island, with the lower halves blue and the upper halves white, and local costume is still worn too. Here, perhaps more than anywhere else in the Aegean, old customs and traditions are faithfully adhered to.

Tiny Kasos, tucked away below Karpathos and the last of the Dodecanese Islands, is famous for its sea caves although, like its bigger neighbour, it also cherishes its ancient dress and customs which are resurrected for various local fairs. The village of Arvanitochori, with its charming stone houses, is split into two by a mountain stream which churns through the middle. There are good but isolated beaches, and visitors should also see the island's walls and the Monastery of Aghios Mamas and Aghios Georgios.

Besides the Dodecanese group, there are five other islands in the north-eastern Aegean which constitute part of what could be called 'Greece in Asia'. These are Limnos, Lesbos, Chios, Samos, and Ikaria.

Limnos is the most northerly and, with its russet-coloured earth, big sandy beaches, and pretty villages, one of the most attractive. It is the site of the ancient city of Poliochne, built before Troy, and the modern harbour at Moudro is the departure point for boat excursions to Thrace, Thasos, Mount Athos, and unattractive Samothraki. In the other port, Mirino, the biggest attraction is the two cinemas, one of them an open-air one for summer use, where Norman Wisdom films have a large local following; there are no queues though, for if the cinema is full the manager simply fetches more chairs from a nearby *taverna* rather than turn away customers.

There are hotels and some nice bungalow developments where visitors can stay, but the interior of the island provides some sharp reminders that tourists are still a source of surprise and amusement. A motorist driving across the island in a mini-car with an inflatable dinghy on top had the uncomfortable experience of watching the workers in the fields pointing and rolling about with mirth at the idea of a car carrying a boat. And meals in some restaurants can prove to be Turkish-style, with everyone eating from the same dish and snatching the tastiest titbits as quickly as they can.

Lesbos, the home of the poetess Sappho whose erotic poems describing the physical effects of love-making on the bodies of young girls were to give the island's name to female homosexuality, was also the home of another great lyric poet, Alcaeus, as well as being the birthplace of Aesop, the storyteller, and the wise man Pittacos. In about 600 B.C. the capital city, Mytilini, was one of the most advanced and civilised cities in the known world, and today it is still a sophisticated spot despite the marks that have been left there by a succession of conquerors.

It is an island of surprises—from the remarkably advanced urban planning of the ancient city of Thermi, where the streets were laid out in fishbone design, to the petrified forest at Sigri with its stone trees fossilised millions of years ago. It is also an island for the Greek gourmet—for on Lesbos, in the waterfront cafes, one can enjoy olives from the trees growing around the Gulf of Gera, fresh sardines and salted anchovies from the sea, and *ouzo* distilled in the southern town of Plomarion.

Mytilini has a Genoese castle in good preservation, the remains of an ancient theatre and a large Turkish town, and a good museum. At Thermi, a spa town, the waters are good for rheumatism. There are attractive island drives, through idyllic scenery, with worthwhile stops at Aghia Paraskevi (there are memorable 'name-day' celebrations here on the penultimate Sunday in May) and Erossos, where there are good mosaics set in the floor of the fifth-century Basjlica of St Andrew. Thirty-six miles to the north of Mytilini is the artists' colony of Mithimna, with its Byzantine fortress and attractive shoreline and beaches. At Mithimna, particularly, one can see how Lesbos has partly thrown off its Sapphic connections and earned another name: 'Island of the Blessed'.

Chios, with its stunning beaches, has a direct ten-hour ferry link with Piraeus and is, with Lesbos, the most frequently visited of this group of islands. It is also one of the ten places which claim to have been the birthplace of Homer, and modern scholastic opinion is that it has the strongest claim although scholars do not differentiate between the villages of Kardamilia and Volissos, both of which claim him as their own. Apart from Homer, Chios's most famous sons are some of the big ship-owning families of Greece, and the island's naval traditions are such that a large percentage of its young men go to sea.

The island capital, after which Chios is named, is a friendly little town crowned by a Genoese castle. Although the beaches are so good, getting to them can prove arduous as the roads are poor. It is worth persevering, however, to get to Nea Moni, where a monastery high in the mountains contains a mosaic depicting the life of Christ that has few equals anywhere in Greece. South of the capital are the mastic villages where a gum collected in crystal form from the terebinth lentisk tree was the original chewing gum. Today the crystals are more often made into a liqueur, or into a sweet, white, sticky jam called *ypovrychion*, which is served by the spoonful in a glass of water. In one of these villages, Pirgion, the women still wear the native costume of a coloured fringed headscarf which indicates their marital status.

Ikaria, one of the lesser-known Greek islands, between Mykonos and Samos, has just been discovered by the tourist vanguard. Its main claims to fame are its pine trees, and the strange goatskin bags—made from the complete skin of a goat and constructed without any stitching at all—which the islanders carry on their backs and in which they transport everything from animal foodstuffs to their own lunch.

The port is small and disappointing, with a stony beach and comparatively expensive accommodation. But catch the bus to the north side of the island, and you enter another world. It is an arduous journey, a three- or four-hour trip over rubble roads and through scrubland and pinewoods—a landscape that occasionally takes on the appearance of a setting for a Wild West movie. Journey's end is Evdilos, a fishing village which is soon to be developed into a proper port. Twenty minutes' walk from the village is the mile-long Campus Beach, which stands in front of a freshwater lagoon and is usually deserted. Connoisseurs complain, however, that the sand is gritty, and arguably the best beach on the island is at Yalliskari, a 45-minute drive from Evdilos. This four-mile crescent of sand is backed by pine trees, and makes a beautiful if lonely spot.

Except in the main port, the villagers on Ikaria are still not used to tourists and the hospitality can be embarrassing. But in return for this hospitality, visitors must sometimes suffer the humiliation of being objects of considerable curiosity. Blonde girls are in great demand among village youths, who want no more than the prestige of having been seen walking or talking with them, while those with the complexion which often goes with red hair may suffer the amusing but undignified scrutiny which an English girl recently received from a rheumy-eyed fisherman at Yalliskari. After peering closely at the girl's features, the fisherman confided in broken English: 'You should go up into the mountains—there is an old woman up there who can fix your face for you.' Hastily grabbing her mirror, the girl was relieved to find that her only blemish was a sun-induced rash of freckles—a condition still looked upon as a deformity in some rural parts of Greece.

Samos, to the east of Ikaria, is also off the usual tourist track and is never crowded even in midsummer. Travellers do not know what they are missing, however, because Samos is among the most beautiful of all the Greek islands. It is also one of the most fertile, and the overriding impression that one gets is of its greeness. Fruit and vegetables grow in abundance and cost next to nothing locally, while the grapes growing on the hillsides go into making a fine range of wines much in demand overseas—even in traditionally wine-producing countries. The dry white wine is best, and can be bought cheaply on Samos; sweet Samos wine is *too* sweet for most tastes.

Dominated by the almost Oriental shape of the 4,720-feet peak of Kerketeos and the Ambolos chain of mountains, Samos is a rugged island despite its fertility. But, unlike most other mountainous regions of Greece, the hills often give way suddenly to green, sheltered plains and valleys.

The capital, Vathi, is a town with a dual personality: modern buildings round the harbour give it a dull, listless appearance, but Upper Vathi, where terraced red-tiled houses climb above the water, is a pretty spot. The town beach at Gangou is clean but uninteresting, and most visitors prefer to head for the island's ancient capital, Pythagorion, an attractive port 10 miles from

Vathi and named after the famous philosopher and mathematician Pythagoras, who—although he has been dead for 2,500 years—survives through his theorem to haunt our schooldays.

There are two superb beaches at Pythagorion, and nearby can be seen the remains of the Temple of Hera, another of antiquity's Seven Wonders of the World. An out-of-the-ordinary excursion at Pythagorion is to the tunnel dug in about 500 B.C. to bring water through a hill. This tunnel, still accessible for part of its length, was never finished, but is thought to have been planned so that it could be dug from both ends simultaneously with the engineers finally meeting in the middle—an extraordinary feat for its time.

There are good museums in both Vathi and Pythagorion, but a third museum in the town of Mytilenioi is perhaps the most fascinating because it contains a unique collection of the fossils of a number of very large animals unearthed in the surrounding countryside and including the fossil of the so-called 'monster of Samos'.

Despite the fact that it is off the tourist beat, Samos has good hotels as well as accommodation available in private homes and monasteries—with the latter compensating for an occasionally somewhat Spartan existence with superb views and cellars of rare old Samos wine which may be offered to visitors. Handicrafts, silk, and pottery are good buys in the shops.

One of the less attractive aspects of this idyllic isle is, however, that because of its proximity to the Turkish coast it is a heavily-manned Greek army base. The troops, who apparently have nothing to do for much of the day, make up for their inactivity by extensive manoeuvres, and these noisy affairs start promptly at seven a.m. to the discomfort of any late-night revellers staying nearby. A more amusing aspect of Greco-Turkish rivalry over the centuries is the explanation for the hundreds of monasteries which litter Samos: the Greeks, fearing a Turkish invasion, have not been slow to recall that the Turks traditionally respect religious ground—a category into which large parts of the island now seem to fall.

12. Crete

Strictly speaking, the land of the Lotus Eaters is in Libya. But, whatever Greek mythology may say, the many followers of the BBC television series of that name know better. For them, *The Lotus Eaters* are the customers of Shepherd's Bar, a fictitious hostelry in the Cretan town of Aghios Nikolaos.

Shepherd's Bar may be fictitious but—fortunately—Aghios Nikolaos is not. It nestles at the foot of rugged mountains 45 miles from Heraklion, the capital of Crete, and it is as beautiful as Heraklion is ugly. 'Port' seems an inappropriate word to apply to Aghios Nikolaos, but it does have a harbour which widens into a lake in the centre of the town. Around the lake are clustered picturesque shops, houses and hotels. It is here, seated at tables by the water's edge, that the local residents spend the warm summer evenings indulging in their favourite occupation: watching the world go by. More accurately, they watch the rest of Aghios Nikolaos go by.

It was at this spot, on just such an evening, that I was introduced to Crete—and as Aghios Nikolaos is growing rapidly in popularity as an inclusive holidays centre, my introduction will no doubt be shared by many British tourists. I had arrived in Heraklion with a friend, a Greek hotelier who had broken her ankle in Athens some days earlier. Because of this, we were met by a chauffeur-driven Mini at the airport, and the Greek driver had set out to prove that it was possible to cover the 45 miles to Aghios Nikolaos in less than an hour despite the fact that much of the journey is along precipitous mountain roads. We drove for a few miles along the flat, uninteresting, coastal plain on the north of the island, and then the road–since greatly improved–twisted sharply inland and upward. In a few moments we were hurtling along roads which at that time saw little traffic, through tiny villages, round tortuous bends, and along gritty unfenced lanes clinging to the mountainsides.

It was a hair-raising experience, and it seemed to go on for ever. Eventually, as darkness fell over the mountains, we saw lights ahead and dropped down into Aghios Nikolaos, where the Mini screeched to a stop outside a harbourside *taverna.* The driver looked proudly at this watch. 'Fifty-five minutes,' he said. 'But I could have done it faster if the lady had not had a bad leg.'

We sat down thankfully at one of the metal-topped tables outside the *taverna* and ordered *ouzo* and *mezethes.* Gradually, we relaxed. The *mezethes* (snacks of red mullet, slices of octopus, olives, goat's cheese, cucumber, and squares of toasted bread) arrived by the plateful, in generous helpings which I liked to think were offered because I was a stranger, but which were more probably due to the fact that by her hotel developments my companion, Mrs Helen Nakou, has brought both fame and prosperity to this part of the island. The *ouzo*, the soft evening air, the jollity of the *taverna*, the shouted greetings between friends, and the holiday feeling imparted by Aghios Nikolaos all helped to soothe town-taut nerves and to emphasise the unique atmosphere of this big, remote, lovely, but sometimes harsh island. It is at moments like this that visitors can fall fatally in love with Crete.

Rested and fortified, one can consider the other attractions of Aghios Nikolaos. Although it has a population of less than 4,000 it is the main town in the eastern section of Crete, and a wonderful touring centre. It is an easy afternoon's drive, for instance, up to Kritsa, where the steep and narrow streets overlook Aghios Nikolaos and the blue waters of the Bay of Mirabello. On the way one should not miss the thirteenth-century church of

Panaghia Kera, with its three aisles and fourteenth-century frescoes; the frescoes, considered to be the finest in Crete, have been lovingly restored by the Byzantine Museum in Heraklion. A stony track which no self-respecting motorist would use, but along which Cretan drivers roar quite cheerfully, leads from Kritsa to the idyllic site of the seventh-century Doric town of Lato.

Lato is a lonely place, as is another beauty spot in the vicinity of Kritsa, the Katharo (literally: clean) Plain. A high plateau ringed by mountains, notable for its clear atmosphere and eerily total silence, the Katharo Plain is one of those rare spots where it is possible to imagine that you are absolutely alone on this planet.

A longer but more dramatic excursion is to Lasithi, and the Plain of the Windmills. A mountain road branching off the main road between Heraklion and Aghios Nikolaos climbs up to the high, fertile plain, where the sails of 10,000 windmills turn silently during the summer months, pumping water on to the potato fields.

En route, you can make the two-hour climb up to the Dictaean Grotto where, according to legend, Zeus was born and where he was hidden so that he would not be eaten by his father, Cronus. The grotto was a place of worship during the Minoan period.

The sails on the windmills of Lasithi are turned by the north winds, or *meltemia*, which blow in Crete during July and August. The *meltemia* do more than water the Plain of Lasithi, however; they make the island's climate agreeable even during the hottest months of the summer, although they do tend to blow the sand around on north-coast beaches. A Cretan summer is a pleasant surprise after the sticky discomfort of Athens, 175 miles to the north.

A suntan comes very quickly indeed in these parts, and many holidaymakers in Crete like to spend a few hours on the beach and then spend the rest of the day touring. That is why towns like Aghios Nikolaos are developing as tourist centres, for on an island 120 miles long, never more than 40 miles wide, and divided into four distinct regions by huge and almost impassable mountain ranges, it is remarkably difficult to get around. The roads can be bad, and it is a pleasant change to take an excursion by sea. From Aghios Nikolaos one can take a boat to the mysterious island of Spinalonga, once a Venetian stronghold and more recently a leper colony. Inside the huge walls of the fortress, Venetian and Turkish buildings remain—and one could easily imagine that ghosts linger here too. Creaking shutters hang loose, and the doors bang in the breeze in the streets where the lepers lived until the 1950s. The island is like a town from which the population has suddenly vanished, and the weeds sprouting from the floors of empty houses proclaim that nature's work of reclamation has begun.

Opposite Spinalonga is the tiny village of Elounda, whose inhabitants were once the deadly enemies of the people of Lato. But today the natives are quite definitely friendly—and they proved it by inviting me to a lunch party at long tables set up in the streets beside the tiny harbour. The Cretans do such things in style; under the benevolent gaze of the village priest, or *papas*, we consumed course after course, washed down with a sweet white local wine, and finishing only as the sun dipped below the horizon. It was a typical example of impromptu hospitality, and one which visitors can share even today in the more remote spots on the island. Such a welcome can be embarrassing, for the hospitality you receive can never be repaid, and even offering to pay for a round of drinks in return may be regarded as an insult. There is no answer to this problem, one must simply enjoy the hospitality and be grateful for it; as the number of tourists increases no doubt it will die away.

Besides its other attractions, Aghios Nikolaos boasts Crete's only two luxury, or 'L'-grade, hotels, the Minos Beach, just outside the town, and the Elounda Beach, situated between Aghios Nikolaos and Elounda. Both are based on a series of bungalows and flats built around a central hotel complex containing such facilities as the reception area, restaurants, bars, lounges, and discothèque; and both are expensive. At Elounda Beach I was again a guest at an impromptu party to celebrate someone's 'name day' (Greeks attach more importance to this, and to fèting someone called George, for example, on St George's Day, than they do to actual birthdays). To the pulsating rhythm of a *bouzouki*, played without the dubious benefits of amplifying equipment. Voula, the wife of a local architect, and one of the musicians sang the light, amusing, yet strangely haunting Cretan *mandinatha* songs, in which the two singers indulge in a 'conversation' made up of couplets played in the same, persistent tempo. To drink there was *raki*, the fiery local spirit which the Cretans deny has anything to do with the Turkish drink of the same name, and which they describe, straight-faced, as the 'Cretan Scotch'.

From Aghios Nikolaos the main road from Heraklion continues, often following the coast, to Sitia, a pleasant port dominated by a Venetian fort and again enlivened by several attractive waterfront *tavernas*. There is a small and recently-excavated Minoan palace at Kato Zakros, high in the hills above Sitia, and on the eastern tip of the island, near Paleokastron, can be found a forest of 5,000 palm trees sloping down to the sea–the only forest of its kind anywhere in Europe. The palm trees are said to have sprung from date stones dropped by Roman soldiers, but whatever the truth of this legend, they are now threatened by local farmers and monks who covet the agricultural land on which the trees grow–and the unique forest is shrinking perceptibly as more and more palms are felled and burned.

The other main town in eastern Crete is Ierapetra, a small port on the south coast but, with 340 days of sunshine a year, a strong claimant for the European sunshine record. Local residents wear short-sleeved shirts all year round, and claim that you can get a suntan at Ierapatra in January. Be that as it may, it is a lively and attractive town, with good restaurants, *tavernas*, and discos, and if one had to hazard a guess at Crete's 'resort of the future' Ierapetra would be hard to dismiss from the list of contenders.

There is good bathing from the rocky coves around the town, and the hippies who 'discovered' the town, and who gather there most summers, are actively discouraged by the police. There are cottages to let—both traditional ones and the far more comfortable modernised variety—in the nearby village of Ayanis Koutsounari (it means 'big rock' in the Cretan dialect, and refers to the Acropolis-like rock behind the village), which is so small that it does not even appear on many maps. You can eat well in Andoni's *taverna*.

Between Sitia and Ierapetra you cross the narrowest part of the island and pass the early Minoan town of Gournia, the ruins of which are scattered over a lonely hillside. It is worth stopping and making the five-minute climb, if only because of the view.

From Ierapetra there is a mountain road across to Ano Vianos, a village surrounded by vineyards and olive groves. This is the real Crete, hard country peopled by stern men who still carry rifles, and by shy self-effacing womenfolk. The Germans found it hard to subdue these parts during the occupation of Greece in the Second World War, and guerrilla fighters who had fled into the mountains that they knew so well used to emerge to attack German outposts. The Germans responded by indulging in wholesale retribution against the villages accused of harbouring guerrillas. There is a memorial at Vianos to victims of the Occupation; other villages in these mountains were completely razed, or else saw the male inhabitants taken as hostages and not infrequently shot. Even today, German visitors cannot expect to be the recipients of traditional Cretan hospitality; unlike so many other European nationalities, the Greeks remember their grudges.

The road continues west to Mires and Tymbaki, past the beautiful archaeological site at Phaistos where a Minoan palace second in importance only to Knossos has been uncovered. Although smaller and less imposing than Knossos, the palace is magnificently situated on a hill overlooking the rich Messara Plain, with the bulk of the Idha Mountains, often snow-capped, looming majestically to the north. There is a tourist pavilion and museum nearby. A short distance from Phaistos, at Aghia Triada, are the ruins of another small Minoan palace thought to have belonged to a local nobleman and again superbly sited.

From Tymbaki, a main road runs east and north to Heraklion, and although the island's modern capital city is not a place which can be recommended for a holiday, it cannot be missed if only because of its crowning attraction: Knossos.

Even if it were not for the archaeological excavations at Knossos, three miles south of the city, Heraklion would not be without interest, however. The fifth largest city in Greece, it is worth touring to see its Venetian fortress (Crete is littered with them), its medieval walls, and the Turkish market-place. The Morosini Fountain, and the Venetian town hall, should also be seen, and it is all set against a magnificent mountain backdrop. But, despite these attractions, Heraklion's very layout can make it seem a dull, lifeless city, and the most important calls must be at its Archaeological and Historical Museums.

The Archaeological Museum is the largest in Greece, with 23 rooms containing a wealth of beautiful exhibits representing the various periods of early Cretan and Minoan civilisation. There is a priceless collection of gold cups, bronze daggers, jewellery, and ingeniously-shaped pottery; while the dazzling frescoes suggest that when it came to graphic art the Minoans were about 3,000 years ahead of their time.

In the Historical Museum there are displays of Cretan national costume, and representations of a typical Cretan home.

But it is Knossos, and its reconstructed Palace of Minos, which tempts almost every holidaymaker in Crete as well as the thousands of cruise passengers who make shore excursions to the site. Because the ruins are so extensive and so complicated—a fact which may have given rise to the legend of its labyrinth—you need to visit them with both a guide and plenty of imagination. The archaeologist, Sir Arthur Evans, did his best to bring Knossos to life, and paid the penalty for it by suffering a barrage of criticism for having gone too far with his reconstruction attempts.

But the reconstructed parts of the Palace, with their blood-red pillars and the triple-storeyed Grand Staircase, bring reality to a site which would otherwise be almost meaningless to the layman. Other things not to miss are the various royal apartments decorated with their famous murals; the extensive and advanced sewage system; the armoury; the royal tomb; the restored Throne Room; the Hall of the Double Axes; and the Queen's Palace complete with its advanced (and still intact) plumbing system.

To tour Knossos properly takes several hours, and it is only fair to say that after hearing so much about it many visitors are disappointed. But it is important to remember just how old Knossos is, the fact that the palace was at the heart of a city of anything between 30,000 and 100,000 people, and just how far ahead of their time the Minoans were culturally. Go to Knossos with an open mind and a little imagination, and you will come away enriched.

The western half of Crete is wilder than the east, and much less frequented by tourists. The main north coast road runs 60 miles west to Rethymnon, Souda with its big military base, and the old island capital of Chania.

Rethymnon is a pretty Venetian port which somehow manages to look as though it is still suffering from the visitation by Turkish pirates who burned it in 1571. Once fortified, it still has vestiges of grandeur. It also has a reputation as the intellectual centre of Crete. But tourists will see it as an attractive town with rows of pretty houses often decorated with iron balconies. *Tavernas* ring the small fishing harbour, while ferry boats use a bigger and far less attractive harbour.

In the purple mountains above the city, at Arkadi, is one of the most emotive spots in Crete: the seventh-century monastery where the running nineteenth-century battle between the Cretans and their Turkish overlords reached an appalling climax on 7 November 1866. During fighting a large number of Cretan men, women and children had taken refuge in the monastery, along with 1,000 monks. A large quantity of explosives was stored in the monastery, and when a strong Turkish force laid siege to the building, the Abbot Gabriel had to make the awful choice between surrender (and probable slaughter) or using the explosives to destroy the monastery. He chose the latter, blowing up not only the monastery and its defenders and refugees, but an estimated 3,000 of the opposing Turks. The incident is still commemorated every year as a national holiday in Crete, and it also gave rise to the motto which is still a Cretan password: 'Freedom or Death'.

There is another strange, but perhaps less dramatic, memorial to the fighting between Cretans and Turks to be found in these mountains. At Vryses, a turning off the coast road leads south across the island to remote Chora Sfakion, one of the spots where the menfolk still favour the traditional Cretan costume of braided jackets, cummerbund, baggy trousers, and knee-length boots. The Turks, and the Germans after them, both found themselves involved in bloody battles when they tried to subdue this area. But one battle in particular has resulted in a very odd after-effect.

Near Chora Sfakion is a Venetian fortress, the Frangokastello, or Frankish Castle, which the Turks decided to turn into a stronghold of their own and where they carried out extensive repairs. The repairs seemed likely to benefit their adversaries more than themselves, for by 1828 Cretan revolutionaries had seized the castle. Under the command of Pasha Moustafa, a strong Turkish force was sent to recapture it, and a Cretan rebel force 386-strong was ordered to abandon the building rather than battle against impossible odds. The Cretan leader, Michalis Daliannis, decided to ignore the order, and he and his men locked themselves inside the Frankish Castle to await the Turks. There was a long and savage battle, and the defenders and the attackers died to a man. And ever since that day, the Frangokastello has witnessed a strange phenomenon that still has not been satisfactorily explained.

Every year, on a day in the second fortnight in May, a little before dawn, when the sea is calm and the atmosphere peaceful, a long row of apparently human shadows, dressed in black and carrying bright weapons, walk or ride on horseback across the plain near the castle, as though they were taking part in military exercises. The phenomenon lasts for about 10 minutes, and has been witnessed by hundreds of people standing on the castle ramparts. But attempts to approach the mysterious figures have never been successful, and they always vanish without trace.

Because they appear early in the morning the Cretans have named these ghostly shadows 'the Drosoulites', or 'those of the dew'. Scientists say, unconvincingly, that the phenomenon is a reflection, or mirage, of a camel train or military exercises on the adjacent coast of North Africa. But the local people will tell you that the Drosoulites are the shadows of Michalis Daliannis and the 385 Cretan fighting men who died with him on that very spot a century and a half ago.

Chania, the former capital Crete, is also its most beautiful city. It began its era of prosperity in 1252, when the Venetians took it over and decided to extend and rebuild what had been a small, cheese-making town. By the seventeenth century it boasted a fine harbour, strong fortifications, and the Kastelli, or old city, on a hill above the harbour. The Turks turned it into the island's capital, and it retained this honour when the island was eventually united with Greece. As a result, it still has many of the grand eighteenth-century buildings which were used as foreign consulates, complete with extensive gardens and avenues of palm trees. Indeed, these gardens, and the town's general air of greenness, have given it the nickname of 'the garden city'.

Today, Chania is two towns: the Kastelli and the other old quarters, and the sprawling new town. The most popular restaurants and *tavernas* are those around the attractive old harbour, while the colourful market is also worth visiting. Parts of the Venetian walls are still standing, with a Xenia hotel actually built into them at one point.

Chania is separated from the huge natural harbour of Souda

Bay, now the town's ferry port and an important naval base, by a pine-covered neck of land leading to the Akrotiri peninsula—a maze of lanes given over partly to the military and visited principally for its memorial to the Cretan statesman, Venizelos. There are several good bathing beaches to the west of Chania, between the city and Maleme, which was the scene of some of the heaviest fighting between the Germans and Allied forces during the 1941 Battle of Crete. The western end of Crete is seldom visited by tourists, and the roads can be very bad, but you can drive across the mountains to Paleochora, where the bathing is excellent.

The most popular excursion from Chania, however, is inland—up on to the precipitous White Mountains and across the marshy Omalos Plain to the head of the ten-mile long Gorge of Samaria, one of the largest crevices of its kind in Europe and a challenging expedition for the fit and adventurous.

There is a tourist pavilion at the head of the gorge, and the rocky climb down to the Libyan Sea takes between six and eight hours. A stream has worn away the rock (avoid the rainy season, or when the snows on the White Mountains are thawing, for the gorge is then impassable), and the path from the village of Samaria cuts down into the crevice until the walls rise sheer above you for hundreds of feet, shutting out the sunlight. At one point the gap narrows to less than nine feet and the rock walls—known at this spot as 'the iron gates'—seem about to crush you. Elsewhere the path is wider, there is thick vegetation and bright wild flowers. Not surprisingly, the gorge is said to be one of the last places in Crete where you may glimpse the wild *agrimi* goat.

Eventually, walkers emerge at the remote village of Aghia Roumeli, where there is a welcome *taverna*, and a decision has to be taken on how to get back. You can telephone Chora Sfakion and hire a *caique*, and look at the site of ancient Tarrha on the outskirts of Aghia Roumeli; you can take the coastal path to Chora Sfakion, which passes the Chapel of St Paul built on the spot where St Paul is said to have come ashore on the island; or you can begin the long hard climb back up the gorge. The latter is not recommended.

The fact that such expeditions on Crete are hard, and hedged with transport difficulties, adds perhaps to their charm as well as protecting the island's remoter attractions from the ravages of the tourist hordes. Crete is an island to savour; a place where you learn a little, leave, and then return for more. And the land of *The Lotus Eaters* is also an island of dreams—an island where, perhaps more than anywhere else, Greece lives up to all its expectations; an island where you can explore when the mood takes you, but where you will probably spend most of your time just lazing in the sun, making great plans, but doing nothing.

The dreamers who do nothing cannot really be criticised. After all . . . that is what lotus eating is all about.

Acknowledgments

My thanks are due to the National Tourist Organisation of Greece, both in Athens and London, for their help and hospitality while I was researching and writing this book. I am grateful to my friend Basil Iatrides, former Director of the Greek Tourist Office in London, and members of the staff for their extensive advice and assistance, and I am particularly indebted to the Acting Director, Miss Cleo Angelopoulou, who arranged several of my visits to Greece and dealt patiently with my frequent and often last-minute changes of plan. Vital information and facilities were also provided by British Airways, Olympic Holidays, and Owners' Services Ltd, and by the following individuals: Diane Cross, John Economou, Reg Fryer, Joy Holmes, Andrew James, Felicity Lowe, Spyros Lychnos, Kevin McCoy, Basil Mantzos, Donald Miller, Cia Moraitou, Helen Nakou, Gladys Nicol, Polly Spentza, John Tranakas, Maureen Walker, and Valerie Webster. Last, but not least, my special thanks go to my wife, Marion, who performed the backbreaking task of translating my unintelligible scrawl into a finished typescript, and to fellow-author Nina Nelson who suggested this book.

The Author and Publishers are grateful to A. F. Kersting for supplying the photographs appearing in this book, with the exception of plates 4, 10 and 11 which were taken by the Author.

Index